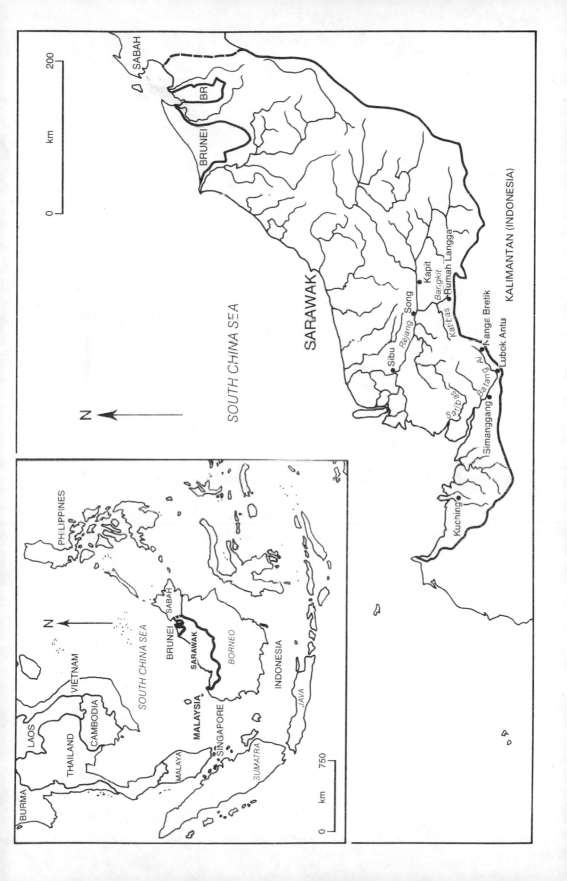

Acknowledgements

I AM GRATEFUL TO The Athlone Press for permission to publish extracts from *Iban Agriculture* by J.D. Freeman, and to Constable for permission to quote from *Good Morning and Good Night* by Ranee Margaret of Sarawak. Tony Howarth's photographs are published with the permission of the Susan Griggs Agency.

I should like to acknowledge a debt of gratitude to the inhabitants of Rumah Langga and Nanga Bretik for their hospitality and their kindness to the wild people who descended upon them.

I have been reminded in writing this book of the generosity with which Dr Michael Heppell and Dr James Masing shared their professional knowledge, and to both I am deeply grateful. This account is written as comedy because no other vein was suitable to the intensity and débâcle of our expedition. It is nevertheless affectionate comedy in which there are neither heroes nor villains, only gods and messengers.

Finally, I should like to thank Time-Life Books Inc., without whom ...

Andro Linklater
March 1990

1

Choosing the Wild People

IN HER AUTOBIOGRAPHY, Margaret Brooke was candid about the shortcomings of her husband, Charles. He had no sense of humour; from the day of their wedding, he begrudged her money for clothes and housekeeping; the rudiments of contraception escaped him; and he insisted on singing *La donna è mobile* off-key after dinner. An outsider might add also that he did not love her, but she never held that against him. He was a bachelor in his forties when they married and, as she admitted with the candour that was her trademark, it was not to be expected that 'I an inexperienced girl of twenty could interest him greatly or evoke from him any great demonstrations of romantic attachment.'

For all that she did not regret marrying him. On the surface he was prosaic in every respect but one, but in that one respect he was romantic to a degree which excused all other faults: Charles Brooke was Rajah of Sarawak.

He had inherited the title in 1868 on the death of his uncle James Brooke, and it was in the following year that he travelled to England to find a bride fertile enough to bear children and wealthy enough to spare the Sarawak treasury the expense of her upkeep.

'Poor dear,' she wrote tolerantly, 'he had not the remotest idea that he was behaving in rather an extraordinary manner, nor had he the foggiest notion of the way in which Englishmen treated their wives. *His one and only thought was the prosperity of*

Sarawak. He had married me, firstly and lastly, because I was young and very healthy and what he wanted above everything else was an heir.'

And so, soon after her nineteenth birthday, she exchanged the familiar background of County balls and presentation at Court for a wooden palace in Kuching, a settlement of houses perched on stilts beside a brown, oozing river in Sarawak. There she was known as the Ranee, but she remained her husband's subject, for he was the absolute ruler of the country's heterogeneous population of Malays, Chinese and a variety of forest-dwellers, such as Dyaks, Kayans and Malanaus.

'Ruler' indeed was too weak a word. In every area of Sarawak life, from the sale of fish to the administration of justice, his touch was felt. He led his country's armies, passed its laws, defined its boundaries, established its structure of government, and left so deep an impression that three-quarters of a century after his death, Sarawak remains to a notable extent the creation of Charles Brooke.

On the map, it is shown as a province of Malaysia, resting just above the equator along the north-west shoulder of Borneo. It is only forty miles wide at its narrowest point, but is ten times as long, and most of it is covered by a sprawling range of hills whose watershed marks the frontier with the Indonesian state of Kalimantan. When Charlie, as the Ranee liked to call him, first came to power, it was no more than a coastal strip nominally belonging to the Sultan of Brunei and threatened by head-hunters from the jungle.

There is no reason to doubt the portrait of his character that his wife painted. He was given to long, bleak silences, and in later life his chilly manner was made freezing by a glass eye which he had to wear following a hunting accident. He bought it, so rumour alleged, from a taxidermist who had intended it for a stuffed albatross, and according to his son the old man possessed 'for ever afterwards the ferocious stare of some strange, solitary marine bird'.

Nevertheless, his passions cannot be doubted either. He

acknowledged seven children by Margaret; the Colonial Office recorded one by a Malay woman, but by far the greatest number of his offspring were borne by delicate-boned Dyak women, one of Sarawak's indigenous peoples and, so far as he could bring himself to admit it, his favourite among them.

'There are many good and even fascinating qualities in Dyak women … sharpness of wit, good commonsense, firmness of purpose,' he wrote. '… Their general conversation is not lacking in wit, and considerable acuteness of perception is evinced, but often accompanied by improper and indecent language of which they are unaware when giving utterance to it.'

And although he forbore to mention it, their skin was smooth and sweet-smelling, their breasts round and long-nippled, and their faces vivid and beautiful. But Brooke's partiality for the Dyaks was not merely sensual. It was their temperament – energetic, restless, enterprising, the antithesis of his own – which attracted him.

In this, the Sea Dyaks, or to give them their modern name, the Iban, were the opposite of their cousins, the settled, paddy-field farming Land Dyaks, who were the most pacific of Sarawak's inhabitants. The Iban remained nomadic jungle-dwellers – their very name meant The Wanderers – and they were following a centuries-old migration from the mountains to the coast when they encountered the power of the White Rajahs.

Nobody knew where they came from originally. The oldest of their genealogies, which stretched back sixteen generations or almost four hundred years, suggested that they began their wandering in Sumatra. So far as the Brookes were concerned they had arrived over the mountains from the centre of Borneo which was then a Dutch colony. They were stockily built, about five feet two inches on average, with cinnamon skins and straight black hair, but they thirsted for land. Each year every family cleared two or three acres of forest to grow rice, and then moved on in search of the virgin jungle which produced the most fertile soil.

Throughout Charles Brooke's life they threatened to disrupt

the peace and harmony of his rule by raiding their neighbours in order to steal their food and their possessions, and what was more valuable still, their heads. Why they first started to reverence the heads they hacked off their enemies was a mystery, but by the time the Brookes met the Iban, a freshly killed, smoke-dried skull was deemed necessary to encourage the rice to grow, to mark the end of a period of mourning, and to promote fertility in barren women. Almost every year, to his death in 1917, the pressing demands of encouraging trade and balancing the budget had to be abandoned in order to mount punitive expeditions against his turbulent subjects. Yet each time he reimposed his authority, he seemed to appreciate more deeply their spirit of adventure. At the age of eighty-eight, he observed with unmis-takable approval, 'What one has to admire in the Dyaks is their vitality, energy and activity; if they are not farming or otherwise employed in peaceful pursuits, they are on mischief bent, worry-ing and killing their so-called enemies.'

Because he found little to criticise in them, he resisted any attempts to change their way of life, other than to punish them for the practices of head-hunting and slavery. In other respects, the law of Sarawak was designed so as to accommodate the Iban's *adat*, or custom law, which was an amalgam of tradition and common sense. Legal niceties did not interest the Rajah. Called upon to try a case involving a couple accused of con-ducting an orgy in a government woodshed, he swept aside the prosecution's case, barking, 'I don't give a damn about their morals. What I want to know is what is the damage to the wood.'

Lawyers were therefore banned from appearing in Iban courts. Although he had to bow to pressure and allow in Christian missionaries, he made no secret of his disapproval of their activi-ties and of anyone else who tried to introduce European ideas.

'We stuff natives with a lot of subjects they don't require to know', he grumbled, 'and try to teach them to become like ourselves, treating them as though they had not one original thought in their possession.'

So great was his authority that long after his death, his successor continued to rule the Iban with the lightest of reins. Only when the Brooke family ceded the country to Britain after the Second World War were the first schools and medical clinics built in Iban areas, and the law more systematically enforced. Yet even then, the majority of Iban living deep in mountainous jungle were scarcely affected.

The consequences of their isolation from the twentieth century have been complex and far-reaching for the Iban, but for me the most striking was that in the 1980s it qualified them for inclusion on Time-Life Books' list of 'People of the Wild'. This was an authoritative catalogue, compiled with the help of museum directors, anthropologists and assorted academic advisers. It included Greenland Eskimos, Amazonian Indians, Himalayan tribesmen and a dozen other examples of, in the words of the prospectus, 'remote peoples who have not yet yielded to the encroaching pressures of the modern world'.

The possibility of selling books about remote peoples had been suggested by the astonishing success of an earlier series called *The World's Wild Places*, which concerned remote places unencroached upon by the modern world except in the form of Time-Life's authors and photographers, together with sundry geographers, film-makers and academic advisers. The books were lavishly illustrated, translated into more than a dozen languages, and marketed with the same hard-nosed, Time-Life professionalism which had made such a success of their forerunners, *The Epic of Flight* and *The Art of Sewing*. Although exact figures were secret, the gross receipts were in the region of £30 million.

Extensive research in the executive salary belts of the industrialised world suggested that remote people might be, in sales terms, 'a little more iffy'. The concept was passed back to teams of editorial advisers who brainstormed it through, and in the end decided it was a risk worth taking. The next step was to recruit for each volume a writer and a photographer who were prepared to live for a time with a selected wild people.

When I heard of this proposition it seemed extraordinarily attractive, and so I sent my name in. My motives were mixed.

At the time I had just signed a lease with the Royal Society for the Protection of Birds for a house on an island off the west coast of Scotland. It was literally a desert island in that it had no other inhabitants, and my first priority was to earn enough money to live there. Not far behind came a fervent desire to go to the Himalayas or to South America. Finally, I was suffering from a cramp induced by too much journalism, and I wanted to return to the wide open spaces of a book. I suspect that any one reason would have been sufficient, for I was not discouraged when I learned that, as though in some geotectonic catastrophe, South America had gone and the Himalayas were being held back.

I was called for an interview on a close, misty April afternoon, moist enough to let the pavement's damp penetrate a tear in the sole of my right shoe, and warm enough to give my one respectable jacket, which was tweed, the qualities of a sauna. The Time-Life offices in Bond Street had a bright, ceramic style. Hard, white lights glinted off metal-framed furniture, and in a honeycomb of cubicles girls in pale blouses gleamed with efficiency. The air was hot and static, and I soon felt trickles of sweat meet rising damp in a fetid mush which threatened to undermine the impression of cool, outdoors reliability I wanted to convey.

Apparently oblivious to the flaws in my performance, the editor, Gillian Boucher, an intelligent, fresh-faced woman with an engaging laugh, spun the globe like Mephistopheles, offering me wild people from every latitude. Discomfort sharpened my imagination. I found that I was not sorry that the muggy Amazonian Indians had been snapped up, but regretted losing the chilly Himalayan tribesmen. By way of compensation, Gillian Boucher suggested Mali, crisp and dry, where the Dogong herded their camels through the Sahelian drought.

It was a tempting proposition. I could taste the invigorating air, see the clear arch of its blue sky, but before I could accept, the uncomfortable prickle at my armpits transferred itself to the pupil of my eye. Abruptly it became a stab of pain and tears blinded me.

'Grit in my contact lens,' I explained, blinking miserably

through the waterfall, and then, as happens, my nose began to stream in sympathy.

It was a shameful display. How could I survive in the wild if I could not withstand the rigours of a London office? The discussion was halted while I leaked and blubbered.

'I think that rather rules out the Dogong,' Gillian said eventually. 'There's an awful lot of dust in the desert.'

I nodded. The globe was rapidly shrinking. No South America, no Himalayas, no desert. In a sudden access of confidence that came from seeing clearly again, I said, 'Don't you have any *comfortable* jungle? Not too hot and with plenty of water to rinse my lenses?'

The answer to that question was the first time I had heard of the Iban.

Although Sarawak's climate was tropical, in the mountainous hinterland where they lived, there was a freshness in the air which was unimaginable at sea level. The jungle which covered most of Borneo flourished here. Despite the destruction of the timber companies which was spreading unchecked through more accessible areas, the Sarawak hills still retained their cover of trees, towering from damp shade into a dense canopy of leaves in the sunlight. The shadows beneath were home to exotic creatures like the orang-utan, the Borneo rhinoceros, and the monitor lizard which grew to the size of a young crocodile. It was also where the Iban lived. In order that they should take their allotted place as the twelfth of Time-Life's wild peoples, a writer, to be precise, an English-speaking writer with two or three months of spare time, was to be sent to live there too. In short, how about the Iban?

Although I knew nothing about the people, I had seen the jungle often enough on television wildlife films, usually presented by David Attenborough squatting in sub-aqueous gloom beneath Gothic arched trees. The more I thought about the darkness and silence and absence of dust, the more appealing it seemed. The Iban came as an unearned bonus, but it was the jungle I chose. The shallowness of my motives could not be disguised, and so I was not disappointed to be told that other writers were being considered; but these candidates must have opted for the desert or life at home, because a few days later I was summoned back. The Iban were mine. The ease of it astonished me. A gritty lens had sent me to the South China Sea; had it been an attack of asthma I might have gone to the high Andes, or athlete's foot could have sent me to the Australian outback. Every disability won a prize. I was intoxicated by a double dose of euphoria – at the thought of being paid to go to the jungle, and at the absurdity of it.

All the resources of Time-Life were now at my disposal and in a gesture that warmed my heart £500 of advance expenses were promptly handed over in a brown envelope that burst at the seams with the effort to contain the wad of used tenners. Experts from the Museum of Mankind were available to brief me, cartographers from Stanford's map shop picked out for me large-scale maps hitherto restricted to military use, specialists in tropical diseases were on hand to vaccinate and inoculate me, a reading list was prepared to enlighten me. All this had to be crammed into three weeks of frenzied activity before we left, and the initial euphoria soon gave way to anxiety about my total ignorance of every aspect of the people I would shortly have to write about.

Handicapped by the pounding beat of yellow fever and cholera microbes in my bloodstream, I tried to work my way through a reading list of eighty-six books. I learned that the Iban were a proto-Malay people. They were brachycephalic. Their society was cognatic or bilateral. This much bounced off my eyeballs. None of them explained why they qualified as wild people. They obviously lived a different life from that of a Time-Life reader in that they were animists, and practised a form of augury from the flight and call of birds which was apparently identical to that employed by King Priam during the siege of Troy. But they were no longer head-hunters, nor was their behaviour particularly violent. So what was it that made them 'wild' or, as I suspected Time-Life were afraid to say, savage or primitive? In short, what was it that distinguished a wild people from anyone else? The nearest I could find to a definition came from the French anthropologist Levy-Brühl who suggested that to a modern mind there was a difference between the material world and the imaginary, while 'the primitive's mentality' saw the world as a single entity. 'To him there is but *one*,' he wrote excitably. '*Every* reality like *every* influence is mystic, and consequently *every* perception is also mystic.' I found the italics particularly convincing. Nevertheless, it was difficult to reconcile this ubiquitous mysticism with their apparent fondness for what Brooke's officers referred to as 'drunks' or all-night drinking sessions.

'A nuisance,' wrote one officer about to join his Iban guests, 'but one must follow out some of these (horrid) old customs however much one may object to them.'

The setting for these drinking sessions and for all Iban social life was the longhouse, a structure variously described as being akin to an American motel, a London terraced street, or a long bungalow on stilts. According to Robert Pringle in *Rajahs and Rebels*, I should not be able to escape the drinking:

'A vigorous tradition of hospitality has come to be a hallmark of longhouse life,' he wrote. '. . . Longhouse-dwellers are typically open and gregarious with foreigners, eager for news of the outside world, and extremely fond of entertaining. There is often dancing and more often drink, and the fun may go on for most of the night.'

However much I read, I found it impossible to visualise the reality behind the words. My anxiety was accentuated by the curious yet familiar discovery that the Iban, of whom I had previously heard nothing, were an open secret to everyone else. A succession of encounters put me in touch with former soldiers, VSO workers, even casual tourists, who had spent time with them, and knew far more than I. As they talked, I realised that the Iban aroused astonishing depths of love in strangers. It was their verve which was so attractive, their sassiness, their confidence, their – the word differed according to the speaker, but the characteristic described was clearly the same.

With increasing unhappiness I began to feel I was an impostor, setting myself up to write a book about them while knowing nothing of even this basic quality. Time-Life, however, had a precise idea of the book I would write. At a series of briefings, I learned that I would write six chapters which would describe the environment, history, religion and farming practices of the Iban, and interspersed with them would be short essays on hunting, fishing and weaving. The central section would be devoted to a great head-hunting festival called the *gawai kenyalang* whose celebration was the supreme achievement of a man's life. A massive publishing and marketing organisation existed throughout the Western world to distribute this information. Over a million people would learn about the Iban through me. And I, it seemed, knew nothing about them except that they might be mystics and they certainly liked drinking.

It was Henry Luce who had brought this giant into being in 1960, the child of *Time* and *Life* magazines, and it bore his unmistakable trademark of catering for people with limited scope for reading. 'People are uninformed', ran *Time*'s motto, 'because no publication has adapted itself to the time which busy men are able to spend simply keeping informed.' Like the magazines, the books were packed with pictures, tightly structured and stuffed with information, and the sprawling world had to be shoehorned in to fit the package. The perceptive Wilfred Sheed remarked of Luce that 'his habit of shaping things into news stories was the real wall between him and reality', and with a little forethought I might have anticipated a similar problem in shaping the Iban to the wild people mould. At the time, however, I was merely overwhelmed by the huge responsibility that had been put upon my shoulders to inform the world.

To avoid revealing my ignorance, I began to pretend to knowledge I never had or, as on a special visit to the Museum of Mankind to study Iban artefacts, to avoid asking questions which might betray me. Generations of Methodist missionaries, rubber traders and colonial administrators must have donated their collections of objects from the East Indies. They were housed in

10

a warehouse among the red brick terraces of Shoreditch, carved wooden masks as ugly as gargoyles, shields tufted with human hair, blankets, anklets and mantles, spears and blowpipes, gongs, drums and cymbals, the trappings of a dozen different cultures from Java to Papua-New Guinea. By rigorously restricting myself to 'How interesting' and 'Yes, of course', I managed to look at masks without discovering what their grotesque features signified, at blowpipes with no idea whether they were used for war or hunting, and at jars, blankets and rings, ignorant of their function or value. Eventually the Assistant Keeper and I approached a cream-coloured filing cabinet.

'I've never had the chance to look at this drawer before,' said the Assistant Keeper with a trace of excitement detectable in her voice. 'Female staff weren't supposed to see what was inside – bad for their morals, I suppose.'

Slowly she pulled the drawer open, and side by side we looked at its contents.

'Well,' she said in some surprise, 'so those are the famous penis pins.'

Some of them could have served as pawns in a chess game – they were about that sort of size – or, given their outline, as miniature dumb-bells. The bulbed ends were sometimes decorated with feathers or bristles so that they looked like gaudy salmon flies, while others were beaded or spiked and could have been used as elfin knobkerries. Their purpose, however, was quite different. These weapons were alleged to have the magic property of turning pain to pleasure and defeat to victory.

'Aha,' I said knowingly, 'the famous penis pins.'

As the Assistant Keeper and I studied their outrageous tufts, their ferocious spikes, the awareness of the circumstances in which they inflicted their wounds gave rise to a strange embarrassment. The atmosphere grew heavy with it. The smallest movement became a suggestive rustle. The air itself turned viscous. At length, the Assistant Keeper straightened her back.

'Goodness,' she said with something of an effort, 'what men do to women.'

11

I chuckled, a jolly, wholesome sound, designed to dispel the embarrassment. It came out as a dry cough which fell upon the silence like dust. Something had to be said, and I spoke a question which I had determined not to ask ever since it began to form itself.

'I don't quite understand how ...' I began, but the Assistant Keeper had roused herself from her torpor and had started to close the drawer.

'Anyway that takes care of them,' she said. And the drawer slammed shut.

My inability to ask the crucial questions – How did they really work? How were they actually pinned on? – had proved fatal. I had a suspicion that they might merely be used as decorations, twisted round the organ like Christmas tree lights, or just possibly as titillating ammunition stuck in the urethra and fired out like a cork from a gun. But the chances were that neither I nor millions of Time-Life readers would ever know.

The sense of inadequacy even included my expenses. They were supposed to pay for mosquito nets, a sleeping bag, a rucksack and other basic equipment needed for a tropical expedition, but the list appeared to have been costed by reference to a Harrod's catalogue. For little more than £300 I was able to buy all the items I required. These included horror masks, pictures of Princess Diana, and tights, all of which had been recommended by Dr Michael Heppell, the Australian anthropologist who was going to accompany us on the expedition. I had only spoken to him on the phone to Melbourne, but by the time I had finished my shopping I was most anxious to meet him. The tights were a prophylactic against leeches, he assured me, Princess Diana would make an acceptable small gift, and he wanted the horror masks for his own purposes.

About a week before we were due to leave, I was invited to a briefing at which I should at last meet the photographer who had been assigned to the Iban. There would be further advice about the conditions we would encounter from the third member of the party, Heppell, and most importantly, we would be told what the book should look like. This then was the crucial part of the Mephistophelian compact.

I was taken to a light airy room I had not seen before. Along the walls were pinned the first photographs sent back by the team covering the Eskimos, Wally Herbert, the Arctic explorer, and the photographer, Bryn Alexander. The centre of the room was dominated by two figures with contrasting morphic outlines – a tall, haggard man with wild eyes, a piratical beard and luxuriant curly hair, who was being talked at from about the level of his breast-pocket by a stocky American who from any angle of view seemed wider than he was tall.

The editor introduced me: the haggard pirate was Tony Howarth, a distinguished photographer and film-maker of almost thirty years' experience who was the other half of the Iban team, and his rotund lecturer was Lou Klein, the designer of the *Peoples of the Wild* series. Black rimmed the features of Lou's face, from the Mexican moustache hooped around his mouth through the frames of his spectacles to the lick of hair across his forehead, and it was immediately apparent, as much from the higher pitch in Gillian Boucher's voice as from the rasping authority in his, where the power lay. In the next hour, Lou laid down the principles which were to dominate the coming months in a manner that was good humoured, but never less than completely certain of the priorities.

'Now pay attention,' he said, once the introductions were complete. 'We've gone to a lot of trouble and spent a lot of money on this project, and we want to be sure you know exactly what we want from you.'

We began with Alexander's stark pictures of the Arctic, sunless scenes of grey sea and bone-white ice occasionally washed scarlet by blood from a slaughtered seal. Despite the desolation, there was nearly always a human being visible, and this was not a matter of chance. Unlike the *Wild Places* series where people were conspicuous by their absence, *Wild People* needed them to appear at every opportunity. And since it was about people resisting the encroachment of the modern world, it was vital to concentrate on the resistance rather than the encroachment. The customers did not want T-shirts saying 'I Love New York' or 'Vorsprung durch Technik'. So, if our subjects were not wearing traditional clothes they should be encouraged to do so.

'You'll find that your people will usually be proud to wear their traditional garb', said Lou with a hint of the Jesuit, 'when they know that's what interests you.'

However, we were not to cheat. If the modern world had encroached too far, we should either find a more traditionally minded community, or try to shoot round the T-shirts. Lou pointed out Alexander's skill in relegating nylon windcheaters, skiddoos and spectacles to the background, while the foreground was occupied by sealskin parkas, dog sledges and handsome, unmyopic faces.

'Your portraits should be very beautiful,' Lou went on. 'We find that people like beautiful faces better. So try to keep freaks out of shot, and shoot your portraits a little below the chin to give the face a forceful look, a little determined perhaps, noble if you can.' He paused, distrusting himself for getting carried away. 'That could give you the cover shot, but remember, you're going to be looking up their nostrils, so for Christ's sake no runny noses. Take some tissues with you, and give the guy a wipe first.'

He wanted dumb shots (full-face portraits) which were not too dumb, 'get them to look at you not the camera'; dead shots (corpses) which were not too morbid, 'we can use them so long as they're not distressing'; and dog shots (dogs) in any pose at all, 'give me as many dogs as you can, we might run a section on them and I don't want to rob dogs from the rest of the book.'

All of this was directed at Tony who nodded impatiently as the list lengthened, and at length interrupted.

'Aerial shots' he asked. 'Can I hire a helicopter for some aerials?'

Lou pursed his lips. They had asked Heppell about the terrain, he said, and Heppell had told them that it could be photographed perfectly well without a helicopter. So, no aerials. Set against the demands being made, it seemed an inconsequential refusal, but it triggered a dislike of the unseen Heppell which poisoned Tony's feelings before they even met.

Although I had already been briefed by Gillian Boucher, I eventually interrupted to ask about the far more onerous job, as it seemed to me, of the writer. Lou looked surprised, then white teeth grinned beneath his horseshoe moustache.

'Your job?' he laughed. 'Your job is to fill up the space between the pictures. I've never met anyone who actually reads the words. Just once I'd like to run a book in the series with only Greek text, and I bet that not a single person would complain.'

I smiled back at him out of sheer relief. My ignorance did not matter. I could confess it. I could shout it from the roof-tops. I know nothing about the Iban. I am about to write a book about them and I know nothing. For the first time in weeks I felt free from anxiety. Who cared where they put their penis pins? Not I, I was only the writer.

Meanwhile I had almost half my expenses untouched in my pocket, and only a week in which to spend them. Of that week I can remember little, and when I was asked to itemise my expenses I found that I could only account for £350. I scarcely hesitated. To the foot of the list I added one final item: 'To living in the style of a Time-Life writer ... £150.'

2

Heated Feelings

ACCORDING TO IBAN LEGEND, when the earth was created it was found to be too big to fit beneath the sky, and to get it into place it had to be crumpled up like a piece of paper. This seemed a plausible explanation for the topographical anarchy that could be seen from the plane's window as we crossed the coast of Sarawak. The coastal plain looked smooth enough between the brown whorls of estuarial rivers, but further inland the country became chaotic. Framed in the small square of glass was a sea of steep-sided, sharp-pointed, razor-backed, jungle-studded, lumber-scarred, rumpled, crumpled hills, and between them a maze of valleys corkscrewing and zigzagging without pattern or regularity. Up here in the sky, all was solid and calm. Meringue-shaped clouds floated in orderly files at exactly the same level as though arranged on an invisible tray, while down below the land raged and tossed in green commotion.

As we stepped from the plane at Kuching, the heat enveloped us with the power of a nightmare. Below those meringuey clouds the air was sodden and turning to steam in the glare of the overhead sun. Reflected off the runway, the simmering bright-ness softened bone and muscle so that the short walk from aircraft steps to terminal was like struggling through ooze. Inside the airport buildings, ferocious notices warned visitors of the death or imprisonment which awaited them for importing drugs or guns, and since at least half the luggage that came from the

16

aircraft's hold seemed to belong to us, the customs officials viewed our approach with grim pleasure.

I was responsible for several rucksacks, bags and canvas hold-alls, as well as one of the typewriters, a tape recorder and a small library of books, but that was merely the writer's equipment. Tony had much the same, and in addition the contents of a decently stocked photographer's studio – lights, reflectors, power sources – together with cameras, lenses and tripods, and also a magnificent medical kit including everything from splints to toothpicks.

Despite my mismanagement of the advance expenses, Time-Life had put me in charge of the expedition's finances, which meant I carried $20,000 Malay in travellers' cheques and $1,500 in local currency hidden in what I hoped were inaccessible places about my person. Putting my signature to slab after slab of $100 cheques induced a Maecenas-like elation, which at Heathrow turned to a correspondingly Scrooge-like despond when excess baggage charges swallowed almost $1,300. Tony, however, became large and expansive. His experience of foreign assignments was far greater than mine, as I learned during the fifteen-hour flight, much of which was occupied with his accounts of past exploits filming nomadic shepherds in the Caucasus and Kikuyu herders in Kenya. His present enthusiasm was to develop a car suitable for the Third World, a project which had almost excluded photography for more than a year. The Iban represented an opportunity to re-establish his international reputation as a feature photographer of the first rank. At the age of fifty such a chance might not recur, and the range of equipment he brought with him was an earnest of his determination to succeed.

To get it all into Sarawak required a couple of permits, another $400 in airport charges, several interviews with officials of varying degrees of seniority, and the expenditure of the small reserve of energy that had survived the walk across the steamy tarmac. Yet despite the hollow exhaustion of jet-lag, the taxi-ride down a concrete highway into Kuching was enough to restore a millionaire's satisfaction. There might be little more than banana plantations and bungalows on stilts to suggest that we were in the land of the Iban, but it was enough to signify that we had unmistakably arrived at the start of the expedition.

When Margaret Brooke first came to Kuching in 1870, the town consisted of the Rajah's fort on one bank of the winding river, and on the other rows of wooden buildings perched on stilts above the mud. Its population was largely composed of Malay nobles, Chinese shopkeepers and Land Dyaks who made a living selling fish and jungle produce. Little more than a quarter of a century had passed since the first of the White Rajahs, James Brooke, had arrived, and the threat posed by Iban head-hunters was still real enough for a rumour of an attack to provoke panic. In fact it was their bloodthirstiness more than anything else which enabled Brooke to establish his rule.

Their raiding parties had begun to prey upon the coastal settlements of Malays and Land Dyaks in the early years of the nineteenth century when their slow migration down the rivers at last brought them to the sea. Encouraged by rival Malay potentates, the Iban from two rivers in particular, the Saribas and the Skrang, took to piracy, raiding the coastal communities from large dugout canoes crammed with warriors. It was their proficiency in this crime that earned them the title Sea Dyaks, and by the 1830s their great dugouts were devastating the entire north-west coast of Borneo.

A Dutch official noted that about a hundred raids had been made within the space of ten or fifteen years: 'they came down all along the coasts in large boats, armed and with about eighty or ninety men, attacking everyone, killing the men and carrying off women and children whom they make slaves ... Their pilots are Malays who always show the way; the spoil is the property of the pilots, the women and children and skulls are the property of the Dyaks. I know of one instance where they killed about 400 ...'

Nominally the traders' settlements and their ships fell under the protection of the Sultan of Brunei, whose rule extended along the entire northern coast, but the incumbent at the time was a half-wit and no help could be looked for from him. Local Malay nobles, however, quickly found that in the Iban's pathological desire for heads they had a weapon which could be primed merely by giving permission to decapitate their enemies; it could then be discharged at villages and settlements, leaving the Malays free to take gold or power as they wished. Rival potentates loaded up with Iban and went on the rampage, and the Sultan himself did no less.

Into the hideous twilight of battle and sudden death stepped the shining figure of James Brooke, and if looks are any guide to destiny he was born to his heroic role. The face revealed by his portrait is Byronic, but while the flowing hair and glistening eye are those of a romantic, the stubborn jaw belongs to a soldier. The only blemish to his perfection was the result of a bullet wound in the groin, suffered as a young man in the service of the East India Company, which allegedly left him impotent.

A small fortune inherited from an uncle laid the foundation for his success. With no legitimate family, or prospect of one, to provide for, he invested the money in a small armed yacht, and in 1839 sailed it to the South China Sea. It was the time and the place for adventurers. In 1819 Stamford Raffles had established the settlement of Singapore on a foundation of energy and courage. Now the merchants there commissioned Brooke to deliver a message to the Sultan of Brunei's viceroy at Kuching. Flying the flag of the Royal Yacht Squadron, Brooke set course for Sarawak and as large a kingdom as any one man could have dreamed of carving out for himself, even in that century of European conquest.

At Kuching, he found the viceroy or rajah, Muda Hasim, engaged in civil war with local Malay chieftains leading Iban levies. In return for a vague promise of a share in Sarawak's government, he put his boat and its guns at Hasim's service to subdue the rebels. Not until the insurrection was quelled did he discover to his fury that Hasim and the Brunei court were also using Iban head-hunters to further their own ends. The largest of their raiding parties was setting out when they saw the muzzles of his cannon aimed at them. Prudently they turned back, but Brooke was now determined to take the government into his own hands. A few months later the same armaments persuaded Muda Hasim that the time had come to transform his vague promise into reality. On 26 September 1841, Brooke recorded in his journal: 'I was declared Rajah and governor of Sarawak amidst the roar of cannons and a general display of flags and banners from the shore and river.'

There was a considerable degree of hypocrisy in Brooke's outrage, for he himself was to use Iban levies habitually in his military operations and, as the Malay nobles did, to reward them by letting them take the heads of his enemies. Nevertheless his change of policy was soon made plain. A noted head-hunter called Matahari came from the Skrang river to discover how Brooke would react if a party of Skrang Iban were to raid his territory. 'My answer was "To enter their country and lay it waste," ' Brooke wrote. 'But he asked me again, "You will give me, your friend, leave to steal a few heads occasionally?" "No" I replied. "You cannot take a single head; you cannot enter the country: and if you or your countrymen do, I will have a hundred Skrang heads for every one you take home." He recurred to this request several times: "just to steal one or two!" as a schoolboy would ask for apples.'

The new Rajah's kingdom, still theoretically held under the Sultan of Brunei, was little more than an enclave around Kuching, but he did not hesitate to carry out his threat. Initially he had help from the Royal Navy which was anxious to suppress piracy in the area, but at the end of the 1840s that assistance was withdrawn. By then he had extended his power one hundred miles along the coast to a point beyond the mouth of the gigantic Rejang river, one of the largest waterways in the world. The pattern of later operations was set on his first expedition against head-hunters from the Skrang, when he was aided by a party of Iban who had previously been their victims. As his influence spread to new areas, their inhabitants came in their turn to join his force against other communities further along the coast. James Brooke was driven by a complex mixture of personal ambition and disinterested belief in the beneficial effects of European civilisation, but the motives of his allies were simple – revenge and the opportunity to take heads with the help of the Rajah's firepower.

Nevertheless, his single most important ally was his reserved and awkward nephew Charles, who arrived in 1854 and spent his first years in Sarawak mopping up resistance in the Skrang. In dealing with head-hunting raids he developed the tactic of using Iban levies which James and the Malay nobles had initiated. Eventually his armies on these punitive expeditions consisted of himself surrounded by a few hundred Malays and several thousand Iban. 'I simply went singly on these expeditions', he explained 'to act as an adviser, and be protected as a queen ant by thousands of workers.'

His military tactics were direct and often brutal. If his forces did not encounter the raiders, they burned down their longhouses, and as he himself acknowledged the result was catastrophic for their inhabitants. 'Twenty-five houses had been sacked and destroyed, some large and some small,' he wrote of an expedition in 1856. 'The amount of property plundered was immense. The ashes of [rice] were in some places four foot deep and continued to smoke and smoulder ... a few hours more and the females will return to weep and wail over the complete loss of all their cherished goods, their heirlooms handed down from generations.'

It was, he insisted, the most effective means of putting a halt to head-hunting. A defeat was either forgotten or aroused the desire for revenge. 'But the burning down of a village, the loss of goods, old relics – such as heads, weapons and jars – and putting the inhabitants to excessive inconvenience – all this fills them with fear and makes them think of the consequences of taking the heads of strangers.'

When the severity of his methods was questioned, he replied roundly, 'Priests may preach, enthusiasts cant, women wail and

21

peacemakers palaver, yet evidence favours the fact that the sword alone clears the path for the sickle and scythe.'

On the other side of the border, sensible Dutch colonial officials looked with amazement at his habit of punishing head-hunters by letting other head-hunters take their heads. They themselves used trained soldiers for the job, and by the late nineteenth century had put an end to the practice. Brooke, however, had no other resources except those of his own kingdom, and ruthless though he was as a war leader, he proved pragmatic and far-sighted as an administrator. The country was divided into five Divisions, each administered by a British Resident with one or more Assistants, aided by Malay chiefs who were often the descendants of the Sultan of Brunei's former officials. Later governments provided a foundation of democracy and several more storeys of administration, but Brooke's mark remained.

Exploring Kuching on the afternoon of our arrival, we found evidence of his handiwork everywhere. In his day, the Malays provided the administrative class, and the Chinese the commercial and business community. Although the capital had grown twenty times larger, the white-pillared government build-ings at the centre were still largely run by Malay officials, and in the spreading tangle of streets by far the largest number of shops had Chinese names. The river too still slid by in brown gloups and whirls, and close to it stood the covered fishmarket with marble slabs and hygienic sluices which Brooke had had built to improve public health.

Behind the fishmarket, a man dressed in shirt and jeans lay stretched out on the ground on his back watched by a few Malays and Chinese. An anthropologist would certainly have recognised him as a brachycephalic specimen of proto-Malay stock, bred no doubt in a cognate society. I recognised him too, but as something much more glamorous, the subject of all eighty-six books on my reading-list, the target of Time-Life's curiosity, the cause of my presence in Sarawak, in short, my first upriver Iban. Kneeling beside him an elderly Chinese was gently tapping a nail into his throat. His object was not to kill but to tattoo. The nail, tipped with blue dye, was tied to the end of a long stick, so that it looked like a Neanderthal dentist's pick. Balancing this device on a board, the old man held the point against the skin, then gently tapped the stick with a small hammer. From below the Iban's jaw, two rows of dark-blue pin-pricks in the outline of a coffin ran down his throat to the hollow at its base. Now the tattooist was filling in the space over the Adam's apple. Tap, tap, tap, like a sparrow pecking putty from a window frame, and with each tap, the point punctured the Iban's skin then bounced back leaving a black bead of blood and dye.

I was aware of the deep satisfaction that comes from seeing the textbooks vindicated. All my reading matter had dwelt upon the fondness of the upriver Iban for tattoos. As young men, they came down to the coast to spend part of every year working in the timber yards and oilfields, on *bejalai*, and a tattoo was supposed to be almost an obligatory souvenir of their experience. Now here it was happening before my eyes, just as they had predicted. This youth already had old designs – stars, fronds and whorls – on his shoulders and legs, but the throat tattoo which was both painful and dangerous was the ultimate challenge. The pain was obvious from the boy's eyes which were wide and glistening, but he made no move or sound as the old man tapped.

We watched in appalled fascination, and in secret relief that here at least was an Iban resisting the modern world's blandishments.

'If kids like that are still ready to get their throats punctured,' Tony said at last, 'there shouldn't be too much trouble finding a longhouse where they still do things in the traditional way.'

The Aurora Hotel where we stayed had a cool, dark diningroom with booths lining one wall, and it was here the next day that we met Dr Michael Heppell. Since he was to be our guide, our mentor, our indispensable source of information concerning the unknown society of the Iban, we were both prepared to dislike him. Tony, who inexplicably blamed him for Time-Life's refusal to hire a helicopter for aerial photographs, had christened him 'Herr Doktor Heppell', and visualised with alarming conviction a Teutonic anthropologist determind at all costs to prevent him from photographing what he wanted.

'I can just hear the Herr Doktor,' he exclaimed, his large eyes looming close to mine. ' "Zhat is verboten, you vill it at vonce shtop, or you vill be shot." ' He ruminated. 'Probably by a firing-squad armed with blowpipes.'

My own fears I kept secret, but they too were in character. How nice would I have to be to Heppell to persuade him to undertake the tedium of endless interpretation? It would not be enough for him to translate the odd sentence or paraphrase a speech; I would also have to get him to ask those crucial journalistic questions, like 'What were your actual feelings as you cut off his head?', that Time-Life needed answering. Direct quotation was the house-style, and Michael would have to be the conduit for their words. Could I get away with ordinary jolly good chaps' niceness, or would it involve some one-sided masochistic fawning, or might we both have to sink deep into a painful, buddy-buddy, psyche-stripping, 'I love yuh Mike' 'I love yuh too kid' intimacy? What hell did the jungle hold?

In the event our collaboration could hardly have started more amiably. At first glance Dr Heppell was reassuringly unlike a German dictator. Balding and bespectacled with a toothy grin, he looked rather mild, and only the fringe of sandy red hair around his oval head gave warning of fires within. Although he had been born in England, it was soon apparent that Australia, the Australia of blunt speaking and anarchic minds, was his spiritual home. Once upon a time he had been an accountant, and the discipline of unemotional assessment was still observable; once upon a time he had been a dark-tied, white-shirted IBM executive, and he retained a driving managerial manner; but as though he were an advertisement for the effects of an especially potent vodka, everything had abruptly changed. He emigrated to Australia, studied to become an anthropologist, and for almost two years lived in a remote Iban longhouse high up on the Batang Ai river. The experience gave rise to a remarkable thesis on Iban family life which amalgamated the usual disciplines of

24

anthropology – genealogies, work pattern analysis, and census-taking – with the more speculative realms of child psychology. It was a strangely sensitive work which suggested that the quondam accountant and new-born Aussie hid another, more complex character.

Unexpectedly a fourth person had been added to the team, Dr James Masing, another anthropologist and, what was of crucial importance, an Iban. He was the first Iban to take a higher degree from a university, and that unique combination of qualities promised to be invaluable. But his greatest asset in my eyes was his capacity to take an electric pleasure in the mundane moment so that it fizzed with possibilities. There must have been a steely purpose to have achieved what he had, but friendliness and a slightly archaic command of English masked it.

'When Mike told me about this job,' he confessed with a smile, 'I said to myself, my gosh these hard-boiled Time-Life types are going to be hard to please, but look at us, by heck we're getting on like a house on fire.'

It was true. We bought each other beer, vouchsafed small but flattering bits of information about ourselves, and exchanged that barbed banter by which English-speaking strangers orient themselves when they first meet.

'Where did you get that la-dee-dah Oxford accent of yours?' Heppell asked me. 'When I heard you on the 'phone, I imagined you must be one of those tall, languid types, but look at you, you're quite small and scruffy.'

'I shrank in the wash,' I said. 'Anyway, you're a bit of a disappointment yourself. Where are those fractured outback vowels, and who stole the corks from your hat?' But he had the better of it.

Over the next two days we ransacked Kuching's shops for the fuel, food and equipment we should need to sustain us while we were away from urban resources. Among the oil lamps, sacks of rice and cotton trousers, the most notable purchase was a gigantic bag containing forty rolls of pale pink lavatory paper. In the only moment of self-consciousness Michael displayed, he insisted that this huge quantity was essential because he possessed the unusual habit of defecating three times a day. My astonishment at his freakish metabolism was not entirely free from envy. A dependable bowel is a great asset away from home.

One shadow hung over these optimistic preparations. In London, the plans which Michael originally suggested to Time-Life had an adventurous air. We should start where the Iban did when they crossed the mountains into Sarawak, on the river they called the Batang Ai. In the late nineteenth century when the spread of Brooke's power effectively corked up their migration towards the sea, many of them had crossed the watershed that divided the Batang Ai from the huge Rejang river on the other side in what was then unknown territory. Michael had suggested that we follow them, trekking across the watershed and down one of the tributaries of the Rejang such as the Katibas river. It was there that we hoped to find a longhouse celebrating the *gawai kenyalang* which was to figure prominently in the book.

Now that we were on the spot, awkward details arose. What would we actually be doing on the Batang Ai? How would Tony's photographic equipment, which had already caused whistles of disbelief, be transported over the hills? Above all, could we be sure of finding Iban living in a traditional manner on the Batang Ai or on the Katibas?

Briskly Michael explained that on the Batang Ai we should be able to familiarise ourselves with Iban customs; it was where he had done the fieldwork for his thesis, and although a fire had destroyed the actual longhouse where he had stayed, leaving seven surviving families struggling to re-establish themselves, he knew the area well enough to show us the salient features of its society. We would probably see a cock-fight and a variety of religious festivals. So far as the trek was concerned, a minimum of photographic equipment must be carried – I could feel Tony bristle. And so long as we were prepared to go upriver, we should still find the traditional way of life being practised. There was a bonus too.

'I'm hoping that an old man called Ngali, who is the last of

26

the great war leaders, will accompany us,' he said enthusiastically. 'And I've got a bard who can chant their sacred songs
to come with us. And there'll be a really good weaver as well.
That's mostly for your benefit, Tony, because it would be useful
to get some decent photographs of Iban weaving. There's never
been a really well illustrated book on Iban art forms.'

It was an imaginative package, but without even looking at
Tony I could guess that this suggestion had taken its place
alongside the rationing of his equipment and the denial of his
helicopter as unwarranted interference in his profession.

This cloud did little to dampen our spirits, and the night before
we left Kuching we had a last celebratory meal in the Sarawak
Club, a foundation as unmistakably Anglican as the cathedral.
It was not simply the white skirts and swinging tennis rackets,
which belonged so evidently to Guildford or Tunbridge Wells, nor
the billiard tables, nor the long bar and its confident, avuncular
barman, but the ringing English in which otherwise soft spoken
Malays hailed each other.

'What are you up to this evening, Mary?' one youth called out
from the hallway. 'You're surely not going to watch those rotten
awful Tottenham Hotspurs on television this evening?'

'Of course I am,' Mary shouted back, 'and I am betting you
ten dollars that the Hotspurs will lift the cup this year.'

We were joined at supper by one of James's friends from school,
a civil servant called Henry. He too was Iban and, although it
was hardly his fault, the party was not a success. With the
Malaysian government's growing emphasis on promoting native
people to high position in the Sarawak administration, both he
and James were assured of power and influence in the future.
Understandably, the subject of our expedition soon gave way to
a wider ranging discussion in which they, and Michael, explored
the political and administrative problems facing their country.
In other circumstances, it would have been fascinating, but here
it induced in me a chilly apprehension.

None of the books I had tried to absorb had made much of the
educated, power-wielding, political Iban. They were not supposed

27

to be high flying civil servants, or to hold PhD's in anthropology. They were head-hunters and rice farmers practising slash-and-burn agriculture in the forest. They discussed auguries and the appeasement of vengeful spirits, not the establishment of a timber resources policy compatible with the maximisation of exports of raw products. Listening to their conversation, I began to suspect that we had arrived a little late on the scene. Tony must have been prey to the same apprehensions, for he looked increasingly despondent.

My gloom became despair when a drunken stranger arrived, claiming to be a secret policeman. I had noticed him earlier listening to us, and although he did not show his card, his behaviour provided quite sufficient proof of his profession. He ordered the breathlessly timid waitress serving our table to fetch him a beer, sent it back on the grounds that it was not cold enough, and kept her running to and fro in a vain attempt to satisfy him until at length we protested at his bullying.

'I am only teasing her, that's all,' he said with an unconvincingly fulsome laugh.

Our interruption served to distract his attention, which focused instead on us. Had we obtained permits for this expedition? he demanded. Did the authorities know that we intended to take photographs? Why had he not been informed? These questions arrived in disjointed form, amid complaints about the service, demands for more beer, and increasingly lengthy silences when he stared sullenly at Tony.

'I could arrest you if you tried to photograph me,' he said eventually.

Hastily Tony assured him that Time-Life's interest in the Iban did not extend to secret policemen. The man relapsed into morose contemplation of his glass until conversation limped into life again. Then he offered up the contents of his dark thoughts. 'And if you resisted arrest,' he said to a startled Tony, 'I would shoot you.'

Gently James pointed out that he was sitting at our table, and this was not really the thing to say to your host. Our guest drank more beer, and the waitress cleared away the kedgeree.

'I know what the law is,' the policeman suddenly stated, as if we had just denied it. He screwed up a bloodshot eye and aimed along his forefinger. 'I could shoot that barman right now, and no one could stop me. I always carry a gun.' He leant back and grinned sloppily at the silence he had created.

With commendable intentions James and Henry set out to show that the guiding principle of the law was justice, which did not allow policemen to shoot people on a whim. The man stared glassily at them, and finally said with only the faintest slur in his voice, 'You know nothing. A policeman can arrest anyone he likes. No one is more powerful than a policeman.' Then his head gradually sank to his chest, and he fell asleep.

Without even thinking about it, I knew that none of this scene would fit Time-Life's version of the Iban. It was my first encounter with my subject, and it was going to be censored. I joined our guest in the oblivion of beer.

The next morning we left Kuching by road for the Batang Ai. The minibus was piled high with our bags, but even so at least half of Tony's and my luggage had had to be jettisoned, and an air of tension reigned inside. By contrast the air outside was sparkling. Towering nimbus and scuds of cottontail clouds floated through a high azure sky, and periodically rattled the roof with downpours which left the red gravelled track and the undergrowth on either side glistening in the sunshine.

To the south, the blue hills which could occasionally be seen above the fronds of banana and coconut trees marked the frontier with Indonesian Kalimantan. The original forest had long ago been cleared, and in its place neat rows of pepper climbed up the hills between plantations of bananas, coconuts and rubber trees. Where the forest had been allowed to grow back, the trunks were no thicker than a man's body, showing that it was little more than ten years old. Some hillsides were covered with a lush, thick weed called *lalang*, which occurred when the soil was exhausted. Only the rapid breakdown of leaves in the tropical heat and moisture of Sarawak's climate keeps the topsoil supplied

29

with nutrients, and unless the trees are allowed to regenerate, the *lalang* invades and chokes all other vegetation.

All this and more came from Michael who, fortunately for me, dispensed information as though he were conducting a seminar. 'Presumably you've read Derek Freeman's article "Severed Heads that Germinate",' he said severely. 'In which case you will know that he argues that the Iban regarded a trophy head as a phallic object. That's to say, they talked of it as though it were filled with seed, and in general treated it as a fertility symbol. If you don't read anyone else', he added, as though sensing the frivolity of my mind, 'you should read Freeman, because he probably understood the Iban better than any other outsider.'

Despite its phallusity, it appeared that the head did not have to be a man's; in fact a woman's or even a child's was usually valued more highly, since the hunter would have had to show a higher degree of courage in stalking close to a strange long-house to find such a victim. But the courage that the head signified was less important than the fecundity.

There was a connection between these murderous beliefs and the invasive *lalang*. What every Iban farmer soon discovered was that the soil where primary forest grew yielded a superb harvest of rice in the first year after the trees were felled, a mediocre crop in the next, and a disastrous crop in the third. By then the soil was so exhausted that even if it were left idle, scarcely enough nutrients remained to enable anything except the toughest weeds to flourish.

The need for primary forest was therefore constant, and provided the spur for the Iban's nomadic existence. As a result, hacking down – of trees as well as any inhabitants encountered on the way – became the essential prerequisite of a successful harvest.

As part of his thesis, James had translated one of the *timang* or sacred songs which told how Singalang Burong, the most important of Iban gods, brought a family's rice seed to them in the skull of their enemy. It sounded a bloodthirsty enough theme as he described it bouncing about in the bus, but its full import only became clear when I read his version in its entirety. There was no difference between the way the song referred to the harvested rice and the body of a dead enemy. One served to describe the other. Thus a verse apparently concerned with successful decapitation –

Behold brain ooze along with layers of fat,
Behold lumps of flesh are strewn on the mat,
Behold hair from human heads is scattered everywhere.
– was in fact a metaphor for the bringing in of the harvest.

It was a sobering thought. In most animist religions, fertility is a property of the harvest god, but amongst the Iban it came from the god of war. A severed head was so fertile, so affirmative, so crammed full of essence that it would not only make the harvest successful, it would also end the sterile period of mourning, and win a young girl's heart.

To nip head-hunting raids in the bud, Charles Brooke situated forts at strategic points on the rivers, and one of the first to be built was Lubok Antu. It was mid-afternoon when we reached the village, and our first sight of it was the fort perched on a hill overlooking the river. It had been made into a post office and public health centre, and its whitewashed walls still conveyed an air of crisp efficiency. The rest of the village, both shops and houses, was built mostly from corrugated iron whose basic colour was black. As the minibus clattered over the metal bridge, Michael pointed down at some long, narrow dugout canoes drawn up on the beach.

'That's what you're going to be travelling in,' he said. His voice had a challenging ring and the reason was obvious. Somehow we were going to have to fit ourselves and our mountains of luggage into two craft no bigger than punts, with hulls made from hollowed-out tree trunks and sides from rough-hewn planks.

From the crowd of Iban, Chinese and Malays which gathered round the minibus as it stopped, two figures detached themselves – a thin man in his thirties with a serious expression on his dark, polished face, and another, chunkier, ten years younger, with a wide grin which revealed two missing front teeth. These

31

were Ading and Ayum, the two boatmen whose skills and outboard engines Michael had hired to take us up the Betang Ai.
The concerned expression on Ading's face proved to be a genuine
indication of his character: he cared deeply about doing things
properly, and the responsibility of looking after unskilled Europeans caused him endless worry. Ayum, on the other hand,
found much of what we did extraordinarily comic, and the
sort of ineptitude which caused Ading such concern made him
chuckle. His jaunty grin only disappeared on the river and in the
forest when he was in charge. They both came from the longhouse called Nanga Bretik where Michael had stayed, and so
they were old friends.

Their presence gave the expedition some concrete reality. Real
Iban, real dugouts, it was all coming to life. Soon there was more.
Michael's culture bearers lived on the Skrang river in a modern
government resettlement scheme some distance from Lubok
Antu, and before we could set off up the Batang Ai we had to
ensure that they would be prepared to join us on the great trek.

The Skrang scheme, as it was called, had been built in the
1970s to house about twenty families whose longhouse near
the border with Kalimantan had been destroyed by Indonesian
insurgents. It consisted of a variety of well-constructed log huts,
each capable of holding from two to a dozen families. In the
largest of them we found almost twenty people waiting to meet
us. It was an awkward meeting. While Michael and the headman,
whose name was Limbang, exchanged desultory remarks, the
rest of us sat silently in two rows on the floor facing each other.
The crucial decision was that of Limbang, and in the greenish
glow of an underpowered neon light the signs seemed unprom-
ising. We had brought a crate of beer which stood between us
depressingly untouched. Occasionally Limbang cast a dis-
passionate look at it as though it were a Time-Life circular. He
was in his early forties, and did not cut an impressive figure. His
hair was grey and receding, and his skin was sallow compared
to Ading's shining bronze. He watched through half-closed eyes
as James and Michael explained our plans, and his tiredly con-

temptuous look seemed to damn us for simpletons. This dispiriting stage ended when Michael got to the point about our Hannibal-like crossing of the mountains to reach the Katibas river. At this Limbang's fatigue vanished in a shout of incredulous laughter, and the crowd's silence gave way to argument and exclamation. There was, it seemed, a cliff to climb, and beyond that a succession of steep hills. On our side too there was comment. Ading slid over to sit between the two lines.

'Who will carry all the baggage?' he demanded, and the wave of his hand encompassed the small mountains of Tony Howarth's camera equipment, the larger mountains of rucksacks and stores, and the two heavy outboard engines. Undaunted, Michael pointed out that the Batang Ali Iban had followed that route in the nineteenth century to reach the Rejang river system. At the prospect of an argument, the crowd began to edge forward until the two lines had curved into a circle. A silver-haired old man pushed himself to the front, speaking rapidly and decisively. He, it appeared, had actually made the journey himself and his information was conclusive. On the far side of the hills beyond the watershed, the rivers down which Michael had hoped to raft our luggage were broken by waterfalls. By now Limbang's face had come to life, his eyes sparkled and he barked out his comments. He made it plain that he would not come overland, but he agreed enthusiastically when Michael suggested an alternative route starting from the Rejang itself and going upstream to explore tributaries like the Katibas and the Bangkit. It was arranged that we should collect him together with the weaver and the bard after we had visited Nanga Bretik. The negotiations had lasted late into the night, and so it was not until the following day that we finally set off on the first stage of our journey up the Batang Ai.

A last flurry of buying added forty kilos of rice and $100 worth of corned beef, spam and cartons of a chocolate drink called Dutch Baby to the gigantic load of rucksacks, suitcases and bags which weighed the two dugouts to their gunwales. I travelled with James and Ayum in the smaller canoe. From his position squatting in the bow, James acted as lookout, spotting the herring-bone ripples in the brown swirl of the river which betrayed shallows beneath the surface, and indicating them with a stab of the finger to Ayum standing with his hand on the throttle of the big outboard in the stern. My job was to do nothing but sit still in the bottom of the boat, and from the level of the butterflies darting across the water watch the curtain of green undergrowth split apart before me. With the sun burning directly overhead, it should have been unbearably hot, but the rush of air in my face was refreshing. As we went further upstream, the arc of sky above me gradually narrowed and trees on either bank began to throw their shadows across the river. Suddenly it seemed incredible, a thought literally beyond the compass of my imagination, that I should be in a dugout canoe, manned by Iban, cutting into the heart of the Sarawak jungle. Yet beneath my hand was the hard reality of a hollowed-out tree trunk, and in my eye the bronzed back of the lookout and the green of the glossy leaves turning to silver where the equatorial sun caught their surface. For most of that journey I tasted a happiness whose flavour never left me while I was in Sarawak.

3

Travelling in the Land of Dreams

Long before we arrived at Nanga Bretik, Michael had impressed upon me the importance of the *bedara* or welcome ritual that awaited us. Once he had plumbed my ignorance, he embarked on an intensive course of education to rectify the worst failings. An early part of this curriculum was to make me responsible for the guest's role in the *bedara*. That is to say, I should have to arrange the offering so that it was in a state fit for the spirits, and to accompany it with a prayer. In order that there should be no mistake, he dictated a suitable invocation for me to learn by heart. It began 'Howa, Howa, Howa' which was roughly equivalent to 'Oy, Oy, Oy'. I was doubtful whether I was the right person to make a prayer which sounded as though it were addressed to taxi-drivers rather than spirits, but it was not something about which I cared to argue. On occasions which involved the Iban, Michael's voice took on that peremptory edge which was once the hallmark of a Victorian governess.

'Don't mumble the opening,' he ordered. 'Remember that you're calling the spirits from deep in the jungle, they may be hunting or fishing, so you've got to make them pay attention.'

Inside my head the *Howa*'s rang deeper and louder, and the prayer's demands for food and wealth resonated fervently. I did want to acquit myself well, not merely to ingratiate myself with

Michael but to make some return for the pleasure I was having.

The further upriver we went, the clearer and narrower grew the river until it could be crossed by leaping from boulder to boulder. Occasionally we stopped at other longhouses, or made detours up sidestreams, but our main highway was the Batang Ai. It was no longer a smooth-flowing waterway but a boisterous mountain stream which tumbled down rapids in short choppy waves and cascaded into tawny pools in white horsetails.

The technique was to aim the prau at the thickest horsetail because that was also the deepest channel, and to open the throttle on the outboard. As the bow reached the foot of the rapid it rose well above the stern, and Ayum would leap to the transom to cut the engine and pull the propeller clear of the rocks just below the surface. At that point everyone took to poling, using ten-foot-long branches freshly hacked from a tree and stripped to make punting poles. I found an inexplicable pleasure in balancing in the prau and pushing it uphill against the fast-running stream. If the heavy hull grounded, the poles were dropped and the canoe had to be dragged like a sledge over the shallows with the river tugging at our legs. It was back-breaking while it lasted, but once up to the next stretch of smooth water we could climb back in and watch the jungle split apart.

Twice kingfishers launched themselves like fragments of rainbow from the shadow of branches hanging across the river. A yellow, starling-sized bulbul darting between a trellis of knotted creepers was more garish, but the pathos of its sweet fluting call could have matched a curlew's. Clumps of pale green bamboo fanned out beside banana plantations grown wild, and tall eighty-foot trees were colonised by fountains of flowers, which had white bells or orange orchid's fronds for petals.

By the time we reached Nanga Bretik, dusk had come to the river, and only the trees at the top of the hills were still in sunlight. It had been built in what was a perfect picnic site, overlooking a flat terrace which dropped away to some smooth rocks and a long clear pool. In the months since the seven families moved here following the fire, they had constructed a bamboo floor supported on wooden stilts, but the roof and walls were made of corrugated iron. It was arranged on what I now recognised as the classic longhouse pattern described in all the books. This consisted of three strips. The outer strip, exposed to the skies, was the platform, some ten or fifteen feet above the ground, where visitors arrived, clothes and pepper were dried, and sacrifices were made. The middle strip was a covered gallery where by day nearly all communal life occurred from mending nets and weaving blankets to gossip and children's games, and where the dogs, fighting cocks and male visitors slept by night. The inner strip which rested against the slope of the hill was divided into private apartments, containing kitchen, bedroom and living-room.

To my relief, once the mountain of luggage had been brought up – 'Those Europeans certainly shit a lot,' someone said in suprise as our forty pink lavatory rolls appeared – it was too late for a *bedara*. We ate by the light of oil and paraffin lamps which gleamed on bronze skins whose shades ranged from polished oak to milky coffee. What they thought of my pink and white blotched complexion and black beard was difficult to tell, but looking at them I felt the apprehension of being utterly foreign. For all the variation in colour and feature, those high cheek-bones, square heads and straight black hair belonged to a single race quite different from mine. The men's shoulders and legs were tattooed and heavy rings had elongated their earlobes to thin loops, and the women wore their sarongs knotted sometimes above the breasts, sometimes round the waist.

Gradually individuals began to detach themselves from the throng. Ayum's father Mujap was the headman or *tuai rumah*, but the centre of vitality was a trio of middle-aged widows, of whom the most energetic was Bangan. When her harsh voice cut through the babble it nearly always produced a burst of appreciative laughter, and her own laugh showed the back of her betel-stained mouth.

It was she who organised the women's fishing expedition the next day, a loud excuse for bawdy jokes. Making a line across the river, they walked downstream beating the water with sticks to drive the fish into a channel made from rocks which led to a large mat laid in the shallows with three of its four edges folded above the surface. When the last edge was lifted, trapping whatever had swum inside, the women carefully raised the mat from the river, let the water drain out, and examined the wriggling, twisting fish.

Bangan looked at their orgasmic jerking for a moment, then turned to the women round her. 'Doesn't that remind you of a man in bed?' she demanded, and before the squall of giggles had died down she threw a disparaging glance at the representatives from Time-Life and posed another delicate question. 'What about that lot? Do you think they would screw like that?'

Had they not been holding on to the mat, most of the women would have fallen over from laughing, and every time they took another look at the increasingly feeble writhing of the fish, they broke into prolonged shrieks and guffaws. But Bangan's racy confidence proved her undoing. Lengths of bamboo were needed to make containers for cooking rice, and when I heard that she was going to take her prau downriver to a suitable clump, I asked to accompany her. Anyone less assured might have had doubts, but she raised no objection. Unlike the heavy craft we had used to transport our goods up from Lubok Antu, her little prau was scarcely wider than a hollowed-out branch. I sat quickly while Bangan deftly poled it downstream, but on the way back with a bundle of green bamboo in the bottom of the boat, I was taken by an irresistible urge to try my hand at poling this minute dugout. It affected me in the same sort of way that the sight of a motor-car affected Toad in *The Wind in the Willows*. At that moment it seemed the most attractive activity in the world, one so satisfying that self-restraint was superfluous, and so atavistic I could share the experience with my most remote ancestors.

Cautiously I eased the spare pole, a crudely hacked stick, out from beneath the bamboo, and with hands gripping either gunwale eased myself to a squat, and from there to a doddering upright stance. At the first movement, Bangan had looked round in alarm and said something which must have meant, 'Sit down you're rocking the boat.'

In my Toadish mood I was not to be put off. We were gliding across the dark pool, the last before the river widened below the longhouse. I dropped in the pole and leaned on it. The prau jerked foward. I staggered back, but was brought up short by a sharp jab in the ribs from the stick. I pushed myself upright long enough to put the point in again. This time the prau slid away to the side leaving me clutching at the pole in a caricature of punting distress. Bangan helped bring the prau back until I could regain my balance. Seizing the opportunity I pushed hard. The prau's forward movement produced a brief stability, but I did not need Bangan's shouts to know that it was all about to end in tears.

In effect, I was balancing on a log, and each movement made it roll so frenziedly that we were certain to capsize if we came to a halt. It was essential to keep moving forward, but we were running out of smooth water. Another convulsive shove brought us to the head of the pool, where the current was channelled swiftly down a rapid from the wide stretch of river above. The first touch of the current was enough to unbalance me. The prau twitched to the left, and I flailed in the opposite direction. In response it jerked to the right and, before I could react, continued to roll smoothly over throwing out, in order of importance, Bangan, two poles, a bundle of bamboo and me.

To say that Bangan was angry would be wrong. Having rescued everything of consequence, she stormed up to the longhouse, dripping with rage. Even from the river I could hear her strident voice denouncing me. In James's gentle translation it did not sound too bad: never, she had exclaimed, never in an entire lifetime spent on the river had she once fallen in until this white, hairy fathead deposited her in the water; that was the English version, but I had heard her voice and seen James's grin, and knew that he had left much unsaid.

Despite this setback, my passion for upriver punting was if

anything inflamed. At the slightest opportunity I would seize a pole and thrust away. I never actually fell in again, but the Iban regarded anyone other than themselves as ineffably clumsy. Either they ordered me to sit down or they physically pushed me to the bottom of the prau, so my chances were rarer than I had hoped. On one or two occasions, however, I think my ancestors and I momentarily brushed fingers.

The evening after I dunked Bangan, the *bedara* was celebrated. Mujap had a gentle smile which conveyed an air of mildness, reinforced by spectacles worn askew and the flapping strands of a torn earlobe. Nevertheless I approached the ritual of summoning the spirits of his longhouse and on his behalf making them an offering with considerable foreboding. There were no spirits of course, naturally, that went without saying, how childish to suppose otherwise. However, no one could miss the numb misery that the fire had left at the heart of the community. If the ritual were badly conducted, say as badly as my punting, it might reduce the morale of the longhouse to suicidal levels. At least that was how I rationalised a rapidly mounting panic as night fell and the lamps ineffectually drove the shadows back to the corners of the longhouse.

Sitting between Mujap and Michael, I faced four rows of saucers placed on a mat. As though at a buffet supper, they contained food suitable for the spirits – glutinous and puffed rice, tobacco leaf, salt, and sireh leaf and betel nut to make a wad of betel. Prompted by Michael, I took from each saucer a pinch of these ingredients and arranged them on a large plate before me: first cakes of glutinous rice which stuck to the fingers and had to be flicked off with the thumb, then ordinary rice which stuck to the glutinous rice on the thumb and had to be rolled off with the fingers, then the tobacco and betel arranged with a hand that now ended in five rice-balls. On top of that went four eggs which were in turn crowned with a cup of *tuak*, a milk-coloured wine brewed from fermented rice.

The five minutes that went into building this concoction were fraught with terror and embarrassment, for it seemed that on one side Mujap with his tired eyes and torn earlobe must be sinking into depths of despair at this inept performance, and on the other, Michael sharply pointing to this ingredient and that evidently felt badly let down, while the circle of Iban beyond the saucers showed by their idle chatter how little they thought of my mediation. Then the sacrificial cock was handed over from the back of the crowd and given to me. This was the moment for my prayer and I was determined to make amends.

'Howa,' I yelled, 'Howa, Howa, nyadi aku minta.' All conversation ceased, and startled faces turned towards me. I waved the cock over Mujap's head and bellowed to the spirits that I had a request to make. I swung the bird over the offering and roared out that I wanted more rice, more food, more money, and with a final sweep of the bemused fowl I shouted that I wanted the entire country to be rich and satisfied.

There was a stunned silence, then to my surprise a burst of applause, in the midst of which Michael snapped, 'Now pull its head off.' Mesmerised by the fury of my incantation I shifted my hold on the cock so that I had its flabby comb and hard beak between my fingers, and tugged. Its startled squawk was echoed by a still more startled one from Mujap who immediately grabbed his precious bird from my grasp. In the awful moment when Michael's laughter told me of his treachery, I experienced the sort of embarrassment that a Japanese tourist might feel when he has been tempted into trying the famous echo in the Reading Room at the British Museum.

My blushes were unnecessary. The cock was merely due to have two feathers plucked from its backside in a symbolic sacrifice, but the attempt to murder it coupled with Mujap's look of alarm clearly struck the audience as inspired comedy. A week later the memory still made Ayum grin with pleasure.

My own feelings were mixed. I should like to pretend that I merely wanted to put on a good show, but the truth was that my superstitions were coming to life. If it was right to do in Rome as the Romans did, then it was no less right in Sarawak to do as the Iban did, and in their animist view of the world, the invisible

41

air was thick with *antu* or spirits and *petara* or gods. Back in the remarkably solid world created by Henry Luce (his imper-meability was a quality Evelyn Waugh found particularly strik-ing, 'densely ignorant' he wrote after each encounter with Luce, '*densely* ignorant'), I had been given an abstract on Iban religion prepared by one of Time-Life's briskly bloused researchers. In her hands, the airy inhabitants of the Iban cosmos took on a weighty, even portly quality.

'*Petara* is used as an honorific for important spirits,' she declared, 'in particular for Singalang Burong, Pulang Gana, and other prominent members of the spirit hierarchy.' In formal terms, the highest power belonged to Singalang Burong who was often pictured as a broad-winged Brahminy Kite wheeling above mankind, and next to him Pulang Gana, the god of the harvest. As befitted their status, neither communicated directly with mortals, but instead sent messengers in the form of birds and animals whose calls and behaviour were auguries of the future.

The other spirits belonged to a lower and, she distinctly sug-gested, anti-social element in the spirit hierarchy. '*Antu* can be both good and evil, though unfriendly spirits are always called *antu*. They are responsible for illness and death.'

None of which was inaccurate, though all of it was misleading. It was not hierarchy that characterised the spirit world, but immediacy. The gods were familiar figures engaged in the same activities of farming and hunting. The Iban treated them robustly as though they were fellow-Iban bound by ties of mutual obli-gation – do this for me and I'll do that for you – although they never doubted who held the whip-hand in the relationship. Nobody foolish enough to neglect the auguries could hope to avoid bad luck. Even closer to hand were the *antu* which inhabited everything, not only the rice, the forest and the river, but manmade objects like the longhouse, an axe-head and a chain-saw. Most *antu* were infinitely capricious, and quite capable of malice, but they could be mollified with offerings, or seduced with gifts, or imprisoned with spells, and some, like the rice spirits, were utterly adorable. They were not unlike the inhabitants of the longhouse.

For the children, the most terrifying spirit was an *indai guru*, or cannibal witch, and exasperated adults sometimes scared naughty children into good behaviour with the threat of being eaten up by her. At Nanga Bretik, they had once had a hideous wooden mask representing the witch for such moments, but it had been burnt in the fire. Its loss became palpable on the evening after the *bedara*, when Michael was gossiping with the three widows. A five-year-old boy kept running in and out of the apartment, and could not be persuaded to settle down.

'What about the *indai guru?*' Michael asked.

One of the widows shouted at the child that the witch would come and eat him up, but it had no effect.

'I think this is the moment for your Hallowe'en mask,' he said to me.

When the child was out of the room, I rummaged through my pack and brought out the hideous piece of latex. Its matted grey locks and staring green eyes produced an ecstasy of delighted horror, and they could hardly wait for the child to misbehave. When he ran in again, Bangan slipped into the kitchen, then came back wearing the mask. To everyone's satisfaction, the culprit almost died of fright when this ferocious *indai guru* appeared unexpectedly round the door, but so too did the other women even though they knew who was behind it. You could never quite be sure with a spirit.

I find it difficult to explain why I found it all so attractive, except to say that the first decade of my life had been spent in the knowledge that the way to appease the ghoul behind the bedroom door was to tap three times on the corridor wall and walk in backwards so that he could get me easily if he wanted. My pockets had been weighed down with lucky pebbles, twisted horeshoe nails and a sea-scoured fragment of green glass. And the only chance of escaping the depredations of a particularly terrifying bully called Duncan was to stare at the sun till it swam with my tears. Everything mattered then, and there were no gaps in the intensity of living.

A whiff of those days must have returned, for without quite being aware of it, I was invaded by lightheartedness. Nor was I alone. James took every opportunity to go hunting or fishing, and Michael visibly relaxed as he gossiped with the widows and came up to date with events since he had left.

I doubt whether Time-Life would have cared much about their writer going native, but their photographer's state of mind was another matter. A writer can always reassemble a scheme from his notes, but the photographer must catch it as it flies, and in consequence even the calmest hum with inner tension on an assignment. Tony had the added difficulty of keeping his cameras dry and working in jungle humidity and river spray, and the physical agony of toting a camera bag on shoulders burned raw by the sun.

Sitting in the prau, I had dressed like Garbo in dark glasses, wide-brimmed hat, long-sleeved shirt and baggy trousers, but Tony was more adventurous. He stripped off his shirt and exposed his milk-white torso to the equatorial sun. By the time we reached Nanga Bretik, the skin on his back was lifting off in opaque blisters from the vermilion flesh.

It was not really a mistake because Michael repeatedly warned him of the danger. It was more in the nature of a challenge to his fifty-year-old body to accomplish what it had done ten or twenty years earlier. Then he had endured far greater extremes of weather following the Bakhtiari nomads as they herded their flocks over 12,000-foot passes in the Caucasus, and later he had found no difficulty in sharing the hard life of the rural Kikuyu in Kenya. Now the years were beginning to catch up. Climbing steep hills in steamy heat, the sweat poured into his eyes; the bamboo slatted floors, designed to support the compact frame of the Iban, cracked beneath his large body; even his calf-length jungle boots proved an impediment since feet had to be unshod inside the longhouse and he had to spend long minutes undoing yards of lacing before he could enter. He was depressed by the ugliness of the corrugated iron structure, and by the men's preference for T-shirts and cotton shorts and the women's habit of pulling their sarongs over their breasts whenever he brought out his camera.

'You don't grow any less sensitive to the feeling of being an intruder,' he said sadly. 'You just hope that when people see that what you're doing is fairly harmless, they will learn to accept the camera as part of the furniture.'

We only had four days at Nanga Bretik, during which the camera remained a novelty, and Tony's gloom steadily deepened. It was impossible not to sympathise with his predicament. What he needed was a scene of remote people resisting the encroachment of the modern world. At great expense, he had been commissioned, sent across the world, and taken to several longhouses deep in the jungle in order to get just such a shot. Yet seen through a camera lens all the signs were that the remote people could not get enough of the modern world. Long before we arrived to take pictures of the Iban back to the West, the Iban had got pictures of Western celebrities like David Bowie and John Paul II. Entire walls of their apartments were lined with their images, and for that matter many others of nowhere near mega-status; in a remote longhouse in the furthermost reaches of the Batang Ai, there was a full-colour poster of Phil Parkes whom I once watched keeping goal for Queen's Park Rangers in the Third Division of the Football League. Outboard engines and chain-saws hung from posts in the gallery. Their kitchens were stocked with bright yellow plastic buckets, aluminium saucepans and tins of Milo, a syrupy night-time drink. All this could be minimised but not the problem of their clothes. Sarongs had replaced short woven skirts for the women, and the men no longer wore the traditional *sirat* or loin-cloth originally woven from bark. They found cotton shorts more convenient, and from their work at the timber camps and oil-fields, they brought back baseball caps and T-shirts advertising Camel cigarettes and such folk beliefs as 'Love is never having to say you're sorry'.

One longhouse we had visited on the way to Nanga Bretik

was celebrating a small festival, which Tony photographed in detail, ingeniously finding angles where T-shirts were in shadow, outboards obscured and the Rolling Stones poster was out of focus. Then in what was surely an age-old, modernity-defying ritual, a parade of girls carrying rice wine came out of an apartment dressed in authentic short skirts with rows of silver coins jingling at their waists. Tony's relief was almost audible as he bent his eye to the view-finder. Then he swore bitterly.

'What do they expect me to do with this?' he demanded of the camera. 'Every one of them is wearing her Maidenform bra.'

There was no way of disguising those flesh-coloured, quilted cones and their elasticated straps. They enclosed the glossy brown breasts like beige tea-cosies. It was clear that we had come to a crisis. We went down to the river bank where the praus were drawn up on the beach, and had an anxious conference about what constituted wild people, and rather more importantly what Time-Life expected them to look like.

I argued that the clothes were irrelevant: if the Iban still genuinely followed their traditional beliefs we should fake the pictures, by persuading some of them to wear traditional costume, on the grounds that this was the best way of showing their inner selves. James, as a wild person himself, took a strictly ontological approach.

'Why do we want to fake it?' he asked. 'Why can't we just photograph the Iban as they are, and say *this* is what they are like?'

This, of course was an unacceptable suggestion, as Tony explained. Although he was not going to fake anything, there was a limit to the amount of modernity Time-Life would accept. Most Iban might prefer Western clothes, but there had to be some who still held to the old ways, and they were the ones Time-Life wanted to emphasise. It was Michael, illustrating the effects of Australian life, who put his finger on the heart of the matter.

'Tits,' he suddenly declared. 'That's what you want. When I talked to Time-Life about the Iban for the first time, I noticed that every time I mentioned tits at the interview, they would try not to smile. If you ask me, I think your photographs need to have lots of tits.'

It may have been meant as a joke, but it made sense. After all, the convention had been long established, not least by the sober-minded *National Geographical* magazine, the very founder of illustrated anthropology, that bare breasts was shorthand for wild people. It was a reasonable assumption, therefore, that in a Western reader's eyes, a certain number of nipples would cancel out an equivalent number of baseball caps and Milo tins. So far the balance was tilted heavily against breasts.

At Nanga Bretik, Tony's mood spread like a miasma. To cheer him up, Michael arranged to spend the day before we left in the jungle in the hope of finding some suitable subjects for him to photograph. There would be birds, butterflies, perhaps even an orang-utan, and he could choose the most spectacular site for one of the farms where the trees would be felled and on our return set alight. Tony looked doubtful, but that might have been the effect of Michael's let's-snap-out-of-it cheeriness.

We left soon after dawn, crossing the river and heading into the mountains which marked the border with Kalimantan. The Iban took the same direct line through the forest that they followed in most matters. They walked straight up precipitous hills without deviating to right or left, and slithered straight down the slope on the far side. We had no choice but to follow them, but while Ading and James raced on in bare feet, our heavy boots skidded on the greasy carpet of leaves covering a clayey soil. Even Ayum who should have been slowed by the weight of Tony's camera bag had to dawdle to stay behind us. Scrambling up the hill on hands and knees, there was only brown to be seen – muddy roots, thick cinnamon-coloured creepers and tawny leaves; the crest was a stride across, and then there was nothing in front but a canopy of green foliage which blocked out the sun and encompassed a still, steamy twilight.

I could hear Tony's lungs gasping for oxygen, and every now and then he called for a halt. As such moments we groomed each other for leeches which at first could be found clinging to boots and trousers but soon decorated shirts and even hats. From twenty or thirty feet away, they detected our presence and undulated along twigs and leaves, moving from hind sucker to front, occasionally stopping to raise their miniature hosepipe bodies and weave their periscope mouths to and fro to catch the scent of human blood. For twenty minutes my pale green, anti-leech tights, fetchingly worn over the trousers, resisted their frenzied attempts at penetration. I watched leeches dropping off trees and others hunching their way up from my boots passionately searching for a way through the nylon mesh, but none succeeded. Then the fish-hook thorns of a rattan creeper caught on my legs, and when I had disentangled them my protection was in shreds. At our next stop I found a knot of four leeches swollen with my blood inside the top of my boot.

There is something admirable about the lengths to which a leech will go to draw your blood. It manages to secrete within its matchstick body anaesthetics which make its incision painless and anti-coagulants so that the blood flows freely. Left alone it continues to gorge until it is as tight and shiny as a blood blister, and pulled away, its bulldog mouth will stay attached to the wound with the redness still flowing through it.

Despite this dedication, the sight of their convulsive movement burrowing into my skin made me retch. It was like a little rape. At first we seared them off with cigarette ends, but this was too slow and soon we scraped them off, as the Iban did, with the *duku* or short farming sword carried for cutting through undergrowth, and with a murderous intensity macerated their bodies against a tree with the flat of the blade. None of this helped cure Tony's gloom, and it reached a nadir when we came upon Ayum staring urgently at a tree. He had caught a glimpse of a creature which had been frightened off by our panting arrival, but he thought it might, just might, have proved to be an orang-utan.

When we left Nanga Bretik, the river was high, and the water surging green beneath the heavy praus made the journey downstream exhilarating. The rapids up which we had poled laboriously were taken at speed going down, the outboards lifted out only as the bow dropped into the race, the poles used only on the bends to prevent the praus slamming into the outside bank. We did not stop until we reached a sidestream called the Delok halfway to Lubok Antu. By rights such good travel should have been preceded by an auspicious dream or the call of one of Singalang Burong's messengers, but when we drifted on to the beach below a large longhouse, it was only the pleasure of speed that lifted our spirits.

Inside the longhouse an old man was waiting for us. He stood no more than five and a half feet tall and his lean frame had been refined to fragility by the withering of muscles. The tattoo at his throat had stretched to scrawniness, and the inelastic skin lay in thin pleats at his waist. Yet even without knowing his name, it would have been impossible to mistake his sense of self-certainty. This was *penghulu* Ngali, the most famous Iban on the Batang Ai. We would need someone to vouch for us on the Katibas, and Ngali's presence alone would do that, but no less crucially he would give us the flavour of the warlike past. The invitation had been issued on our way upstream, and now we should know the answer.

Ngali led us to the mat outside his apartment, and offered some weak *tuak*. After some idle conversation, Michael asked him the crucial question, had he had a dream?

'Yes, I had a dream,' he replied, 'just a small dream, a tiny little dream.'

His eyes, milky with old age, were shining and his seamed cheeks bulged with pleasure. In the shadowy light of the long-house he looked half his eighty-odd years. He peered closely at us, and when he saw that he had our attention, he pouched the wad of betel he had been chewing. 'This is what I dreamed,' he began.

His entire life had been studded with great events foretold by dreams. His very reputation sprang from the images which appeared while he slept. At the age of seven in the last years of Charles Brooke's long reign, he dreamed that he was present at a

49

gathering of Iban leaders from hundreds of longhouses presided over by a powerful white commander. It was such a significant scene – quite inappropriate for a child – that his father told him to keep it a secret otherwise he would be teased as a boaster. Whether the dreams gave a person the confidence to achieve them, or innate confidence produced auspicious dreams, is a moot point, but the fact was that even in his twenties the authority of his personality enabled him to exercise influence far beyond his own longhouse. And so when Vyner Brooke, Charles's son and successor as Rajah, called an assembly of Iban headmen from the Batang Ai to make peace between the upriver and downriver factions, the young Ngali was among those summoned to attend.

Except in his bearing there was little to suggest the man he was, but in the stories of his youth it was the speed of hand and brain and the decisiveness which people remembered. Even in his sixties he had still thought nothing of descending on a nearby longhouse and abducting a twenty-year-old girl who became his fourth wife. When the Japanese invaded Sarawak in 1941, he was one of the few Iban leaders to dispute their claim to rule, and on the Allies' return in 1945 he and another river hero called Jimbun led an army of 6,000 Iban against the Japanese garrison in Lubok Antu. As they swept down the hill he was felled by a machine-gun bullet which hit him in the leg. Defiantly he got back on his feet and shouted, 'Look, these Japanese bullets are harmless. They can't hurt us. Come on.' After which nothing could stop them, and they poured into the village driving out the enemy.

A dream was a message from the unseen world of gods and spirits, and it was by heeding them that Ngali had been able to carve his life in heroic proportions. If he were to accompany us, he would first need to have seen some kind of portent during the night. Unless it was favourable, we should travel on alone.

'I was fishing,' he said, 'and I cast my net in the pool again and again but caught nothing. I decided to inspect my fish-trap, and there I found a gigantic *enkenkali* fish [this can weigh up to sixty pounds]. For a long time I had to wrestle with it in the

50

fish-trap, and at last I drew my *duku* and killed it.'

He sat back with an air of triumph. It was incontestably a good dream. Not only had his fishing been successful, his spirit had shown itself ready to struggle hard and persistently, and that was the best sign of all. By itself an auspicious dream could only point the way to success – to achieve it demanded unremitting effort as well.

Our own dreamlessness might have been a warning to proceed with caution, but as small components of a gigantic marketing and publishing enterprise, our dream-life or lack of it could not stand in the way of bringing back the story. That was our excuse for travelling, but Ngali's was more complicated. Ostensibly his interest in joining us was to visit relatives, including his sister who had migrated to the Katibas river, but more compelling than family concerns was the simple urge to go on *bejalai* or a journey.

It was an itch from which every male Iban suffered. The longhouse was one pole of their existence, but its opposite pole was travel. The greater part of a young man's early adulthood was spent away from home, travelling for work or for trade or simply for excitement. At quiet periods in the farming cycle, whole families went on the move visiting friends and relatives To be an Iban was to have a lust for wandering, and their very name, which was derived from a Kayan word, *hivan*, meaning to wander, recognised the fact.

Wearing a blue Homburg and a dun-coloured windcheater, Ngali took his place in the centre of Ading's prau, sitting very straight and staring fixedly ahead. Since we could not follow the mountain and river route of the Batang Ai Iban, we had to adopt more conventional means of transport, and at Lubok Antu we unloaded our luggage from the praus into a bus. On the way we picked up Limbang, now fizzing with energy, and his two artists, Inyang the weaver, and Danggang the bard.

In any culture Inyang's strong face and direct look would have stamped her as a forceful personality. But for the Iban there was a more obvious sign: the backs of her hands were tattooed dark

51

blue, from the first joint of the finger to her wrist. The only other people I had seen with such markings were two men who had taken part in a successful ambush on an Indonesian patrol in the confrontation of the 1960s, and a third who had acted as a scout for British troops in Malaya in the 1950s. On them the tattoos meant that they had successfully brought home a head. Inyang had earned hers in a more subtle way.

What gave a head its value was its spirit which now belonged to its new owner. A weaver could capture spirits too, but the undertaking was not easy. There was power in an image, whether it represented a person or a quality like courage or fertility. Before work began, it required the sanction of a dream, and its execution demanded the determination of a warrior if the capricious spirit was to be held; to prevent it escaping, the design always incorporated a densely woven, layered border. Offerings had to be made and rituals observed, but when the masterpiece was complete, the weaver commanded the same public esteem as a head-hunter. Inyang could be very funny, especially teasing Danggang, but fundamentally she was *une femme sérieuse*.

Danggang's teasability was at once apparent. In contrast to most of his countrymen he was slightly built and his clumsiness made him giggle self-deprecatingly when asked to navigate or help with the poling. There was equally little risk of mistaking his intelligence. Paris intellectuals in the fifties used to have his sharp-featured, beaky-nosed look, a resemblance heightened by his quick grin and animated expression once his attention was engaged. Yet even then, his near toothless mouth and nasal voice made it difficult to believe that anyone would be beguiled by his words. Only experience revealed his true gifts.

The journey to the Rejang river consumed most of a hot bumpy day, which seemed long enough but was short by comparison with the generations taken by the Iban migrants. Our destination was Sibu, Sarawak's second largest city, and a major port near the mouth of the mile-wide Rejang river. Its character had been irrevocably forged by Charles Brooke who encouraged the immigration of large numbers of Christian Foochow Chinese in the early years of the twentieth century. Their success as rubber planters and their entrepreneurial flair initially provided the impoverished state with much of its revenue, but for a time their immigration became too much of a good thing, for when rubber prices boomed before the First World War, they flooded into the Sibu area dispossessing Iban farmers of their land. Nevertheless, the long rows of shops and small businesses, the gigantic office blocks and the fleets of boats, large and small, all bearing Chinese names, provided a forcible reminder of the Rajah's vision and zest for social engineering.

Another tangible souvenir of his rule struck me as we waited at the dockside for a ferry to take us upriver to the village of Ngemah where we could hire praus suitable for the smaller tributaries like the Katibas and the Bangkit. The ferries were steel-hulled launches which battered their way into the landing-stage like gigantic pigs jostling at the trough. There they were promptly overrun by a crowd of Iban and Chinese traders waiting to get upriver. In the midst of the waiting crowds, my attention was caught by an old man, dressed in sandals, tattered shorts and buttonless shirt, who was selling pineapples or, as it appeared, daring people to buy them. His skin was pale copper, but he stood much taller than the average Iban, and his cold grey eyes stared disdainfully at his customers down a high-bridged, aquiline nose.

The sudden blare of a ferry siren distracted me, and I was thrown into the scrum needed to get our luggage on board. Soon afterwards the ferry's engines revved up, and the deafening roar of twin diesels at nearly full power punctuated by the concussive thud of hull hitting hull as we reversed away from the dock and into the river drove out the startling impression created by the pineapple-seller's face. We were an hour out of Sibu before I understood what was remarkable about the old man – he was Rajah Charles Brooke to the life.

In his early memoirs, *Ten Years in Sarawak*, Brooke's references to the physical beauty of young Iban girls are suffused with sensuality; 'In youth and before marriage their figures are slight and graceful, with small waists, and not too largely developed to obliterate the sylph-like contour of a budding beauty. Their eyes are, in most cases, jet black, clear and bright, with quick intelligence and temper beaming through the orbs. The shape of the lid when open is very oval, the lashes long and thick.... They seldom fail to shake their heads before a spectator, in order to toss their flowing tresses over their back and shoulders. The more favoured ones, too, when on a visit, are fond of the excuse of excessive heat requiring the jacket to be withdrawn, to expose a smooth, satiny, brown skin.'

Unlike some of his officers who treated their Iban mistresses as conveniences – one merely referred to her as 'my bitch' – Brooke's feelings ran to fierce jealousy. According to his wife he took violent revenge when he discovered that one of his mistresses at Simanggang had been unfaithful with a soldier at the fort; 'He had her head shaved, and tied the thick long tail of hair to the flag staff!! Then she was put in a boat, shaven and shorn, and paddled to and fro in front of the company with a man who summoned the people to the bank by a gong, and who informed the populace of her misdeeds.' What happened to the soldier was not recounted.

The pineapple-seller was, I estimated, in his seventies, and although the odds might be against it he must have been the result of a late fling by the old Rajah, perhaps when he came to Sibu in 1915 to direct the last great punitive expedition of his life. At the time Brooke reckoned that he had personally commanded fifty such retaliatory raids – an average of one for each year of his reign – and to the end he supervised their planning in detail. In that respect at least his powers were undiminished, and to judge by his correspondence he remained vigorous and dominating in character. To have fathered one more child was not beyond him even at the age of eighty-five.

His other legacies were more substantial. He preserved, sometimes unwittingly but more often consciously, Iban traditions, and of equal importance brought them to the point of recognising themselves as Iban rather than as isolated river-dwellers. At the same time the commercial bustle of Sibu was his doing, as were the whitewashed fort at Lubok Antu, the administrative Divisions, the system of *penghulu*, and a myriad other continuing aspects of government. And by the Iban he was regarded as the greatest of all war leaders, a figure of such power that even today a white skin has something of the capricious force of an *antu* or spirit, and remains sufficiently terrifying at least to silence a noisy child. In every sense of the word, he was the Father of Sarawak.

These speculations occurred sporadically as I lay among our baggage on the roof of the ferry. The Rejang is one of the largest rivers in the world; over a hundred miles from the sea it is still almost half a mile wide, and coasters of several hundred tons plough heavily through the earth-brown water. They occupied the centre of the river, but the ferry hugged the bank to keep out of the current. Periodically we wheeled like a swallow across the stream to a landing-stage on the far side where we nosed in, engines still running to hold the boat against the stream until passengers laden with baskets of fruit and boxes of machinery had scrambled on and off. Minutes later we backed away, and the impassive Chinese skipper opened the throttle wide once more. Sitting inside the cabin, the howl of the engines was deafening and the continuous cascades of water flung up on either side hid the view. But up on the roof, the warm air swept your face while the country slowly changed from mangrove swamp to the familiar forested hills, and the grey weight of cloud above dwindled to a few white ruffles in a blue sky.

This interlude of idleness ended at Ngemah where our belongings had to be flung ashore in the same frenzy that they had been loaded. Another government scheme for Iban had been established here, with about three hundred families living in longhouses close to rubber plantations and pepper farms. With some difficulty we hired three praus, and an extra engine which Tony expertly stripped down and overhauled. The dugouts were bigger and heavier than the ones on the Batang Ai, and they held our enlarged party with little difficulty. Two hours up the Rejang, we turned into the mouth of the Katibas, a swirling, tawny river swollen by recent rains. Fortunately the high level of the river made navigation easier, and a few hours more brought us to the mouth of the Bangkit, a dark green stream which emerged from beneath overhanging boughs.

Ngali had been rather withdrawn during the journey. His blue hat still square on his head, he sat silent and aloof as we continued upstream. Now he motioned us to go up the Bangkit. A little later we passed a flight of steps coming down the bank to a deep pool. From the river the only other visible signs of human habitation were the uppermost leaves of a grove of fruit trees. This was where Ngali's relatives lived. We pulled in to the bank and climbed the steps to find a big longhouse set back in a clearing. Ngali led us up the ladder and into the gallery. Two girls were pounding rice at one end, and the walls and beams were white with the accumulation of years of rice dust. A man was knotting a fishing net suspended from a beam, and in the centre of the floor a grey-haired man chewing betel nut sat beside an old woman who was splitting rattan.

Without hesitation Ngali approached the old woman and peremptorily demanded, 'Why haven't you put out a decent mat for me?'

The old woman looked up in astonishment, obviously not knowing who he was. 'I didn't know you were coming', she said courteously, 'otherwise I would have laid out mats to the door.'

Hardly mollified, Ngali waited while rattan mats were pulled down from the beams and rolled out on the floor. When we had all sat down, he looked sternly at the woman who was now surrounded by people attracted by our arrival.

'Where do you come from?' she asked as was only polite.

'From the Batang Ai,' Ngali snapped impatiently.

They all nodded with interest, for most of the Bangkit families originally came from there.

Ngali glared at them. 'Don't you know who I am?' he shouted.

Deeply embarrassed but determined to humour this fierce old man, they all hurriedly assured him that of course they knew who he was, no one could fail to recognise him, but just at the moment . . .

'I am Ngali from Delok,' he declared in ringing tones.

It was like a spell which awoke them with a start from the grip of their embarrassment. The old woman seized his hand and stared into his face with wonder. Her husband, the grey-haired man, took Ngali's other hand and beamed at him. The onlookers leaped into action. The women ran back to their apartments to tell relatives and fetch *tuak*. The men shouted the news along the gallery and out on to the platform. Everywhere in the flood of Iban came the word, 'Ngali', 'Ngali'. Suddenly a door flew open and a wrinkled old woman with grey hair hanging down to her breasts ran out and kneeling by his side grasped his hand. Her wide mouth, lipstick-red with betel juice, puckered uncontrollably. Unable to speak, she could only gaze silently at her brother while the tears streamed down her cheeks. Almost gently Ngali drew her to her feet and let himself be led away to her apartment.

We were a large party, too much for one household, and so we were divided up to spread our store of information and our thirst. Once word got around that we were searching for a longhouse which was planning to hold a *gawai kenyalang*, several possibilities were suggested. At the top of the Bangkit, a large longhouse was celebrating one, but that might already have begun. More promising was the longhouse below it, where a family had been making preparations for some time, and was expected to begin their festival shortly. This news was enough to make us anxious to continue, but it was late in the day before we left, drunk with emotion and *tuak*. Ngali himself took it all with unshaken dignity, although his mood had perceptibly mellowed.

He was after all a famous man accustomed to receive attention throughout his adult life, and aware from the earliest days that he was something out of the ordinary. In a sense he was an anachronism. Of Sarawak's 320,000 Iban, only a minority still lived in the *ulu*, the upper reaches of the country's rivers, their lives hardly altered in their essentials since Charles Brooke's death, but of them Ngali might be taken as the beau ideal.

Almost a quarter of a century had passed since the last Iban war-party went on the march, but as though his life were a microcosm of recent Iban history, Ngali was deeply involved. No blood was spilled in the affair known as The War of the Penises, but so splendidly titled a war deserves a place in history. It certainly has a place in Iban memory. When we arrived at Rumah Langga, the longhouse where the *gawai kenyalang* was being planned, the men sat up late re-fighting the whole episode.

Like most Iban feuds it built up from small beginnings, and the course it followed was so traditional that the Brookes and their colonial regimes might never have existed. It started when a half-blind boy from the Batang Ai was sent to collect a basket from Badau, a longhouse across the border in Kalimantan. While he was there some girls started to tease him, and the boldest of them pulled up her skirt in front of him, mocking his lack of sight.

'I asked why everyone was laughing,' he explained to us when, much later, we met him, 'and they told me what she was doing.'

The next day two youths began to bully him, and in his confusion their victim shouted out that he had seen the girl's vagina. He could hardly have done anything more terrible short of taking her head, for the Iban are excessively modest about their private parts. Infuriated by the insult to their longhouse, the young men beat him up, and one of them, called Langgai, exclaimed, 'You're not worth fighting. Tell your father to come and fight, and if he doesn't come, I'll know the Batang Ai men have no penises. You tell them they have no penises.'

The blind boy returned home and duly passed on the message to Ngali and Jimbun, and they followed *adat* or custom law by calling a meeting of all the Batang Ai headmen to decide what should be done. Most at once called for a full war-party with heads to be taken. When the two war leaders counselled against the head-hunting, many refused to come at all. Even so, four hundred men from the Batang Ai, including Ading and Limbang, followed Ngali and Jimbun across the border into Kalimantan. A mile short of Badau, the leaders halted their band and again warned them against taking heads. They were simply going to extract a fine for the insult and the assault.

'Oh, in that case it's just women's work,' Limbang protested and left in disgust.

The leaders marched up to the longhouse and shouted, 'The Batang Ai penises have arrived. Why don't you come out and take a look at them?'

At first there was utter silence in the longhouse, then the blind boy's father lost patience and rushing forward into the space beneath the longhouse fired his shotgun up through the floor. At once pandemonium broke out. The Batang Ai men systematically laid waste to the land round the longhouse, cutting down the fruit trees, slaughtering the livestock, destroying the pepper gardens and burning nearby huts. As they did so, the women in the longhouse ran out on to the platform screaming that they would submit, and waving fighting cocks in the air as a sign of surrender. They were followed by the headman who explained in a trembling voice that Langgai had fled, although at that moment he was in fact hiding in a rice bin. In due course, there was a formal act of submission, an offering was made to the gods, and two Chinese jars and two gongs were handed over in compensation for the insult. For good measure, Ngali then fined each family $50 Malay, before leading his band away.

That should have been the end of it, but there was a sequel, and it was the sequel that Ngali most enjoyed. Within hours, news of their attack had been taken to Budit, the most powerful leader of the Kalimantan Iban, and over 1,000 men at once followed him in pursuit of Ngali. Word of the impending conflict sent a British colonial officer hurrying up to Lubok Antu where he found the two forces ready for battle just outside the town.

Ngali's eyes brightened as he told how the officer had attempted to make peace between the two leaders. Budit was prepared to be conciliatory. The return of the jars, the gongs and the money, together with a fine for the damage would be sufficient for him. Ngali was having none of it.

'I showed him my arse,' he declared angrily. ' "If you want to curse me," I said, "here I am. My home is at Delok and my name is Ngali." ' His fierce hawk's head lifted defiantly, and he glared at his audience as though they were Budit. ' "If you want fines," I told him, "I've got enough jars and gongs for any number of fines",' a pause while he shifted his wad of betel, ' "all you've got to do is come and get them." '

There were grunts of appreciation from his listeners – that was the way to behave – and Ngali nodded vigorously, as though approving the words of his younger self. He did not choose to explain that the Chinese shopkeepers, alarmed at the thought of the damage which a battle might cause, then collected enough money to satisfy Budit's claims, and that with their pride intact the Kalimantan Iban had returned to their side of the border. The cream of the episode so far as he was concerned came with the reaction of the British officer.

'He shouted at me,' Ngali said with satisfaction. ' "You silly little boy," he shouted, "you don't understand what you've been doing." And he picked me up and shook me.' The memory made him laugh. 'Then he said, "Listen to me, I know the history of America, of England, of Holland, and two other countries whose names I don't remember, but this thing you've done is the biggest wrong I have ever heard of".' Ngali leaned back with a smile across his face. It was an accolade to warm the chill of old age.

One of his audience ventured to suggest that the government had grounds for being a little upset, but Ngali replied as a hero should. 'If I had done something by myself, it would have been wrong, but I had four hundred men with me – that shows I was right.'

The long gallery was dark now, but for the glow of some oil-lamps which lit the forms of sleeping bodies and the dozen or so faces turned towards Ngali. He himself was tired, and his face began to go dull with weariness. It was time to sum up.

'Other people have lost battles,' he said. 'I haven't – so far.' He leaned over and spat his betel through a slat in the floor. 'I've been lucky.'

Someone in the audience coughed in disagreement. 'When men are brave,' he said, 'the gods favour their actions.'

Then one by one the listeners stood up and went to bed, leaving the old man to stretch his body out on the floor and dream great dreams.

4

The Wanton Praise-Singer

THE ONLY DREAM of note I had in Sarawak occurred in the government longhouse scheme at Ngemah. It was incontestably a bad omen. I dreamed that a black poodle was biting my throat, and awoke to find my mosquito net wrapped around my neck and all the dogs in the scheme howling. At a rough estimate, the scheme consisted of twenty longhouses, each longhouse held about fifteen families, and each family owned about five dogs ... while I still grappled with midnight arithmetic, they all gave voice again ... fifteen hundred, I finally calculated, canine sirens producing a soup-like soprano warning of witches, sudden murder and evil spirits. At Rumah Langga there were fewer than fifty dogs, but the prejudice born at Ngemah only grew more bitter.

Throughout the night in the long gallery where unmarried men and male visitors slept, the dogs scrabbled and fought; they growled menacingly, yelped submissively and scratched obsessively. The drumroll of scratching hindquarters hitting a wooden floor would have made a tympanist envious, but when the floor was made from split bamboo the vibrations turned your bed into a trampoline. Michael armed himself with the long stick which our hosts had thoughtfully left out for the purpose, and periodically there was a smack and a squeal and a brief silence. It did not last long enough for sleep to return.

While the sky was still dark, the pigs awoke in the mud

beneath the longhouse, and the discomfort of lying restlessly on a thin rattan mat was underlined by the leisurely squelching and satisfied geromph-geromphing from below. Soon the discovery of some garbage in the ooze produced a chorus of excited snorts, interrupted by the oinks of a frustrated latecomer. The snorters oinked back, the oinkers began to squeal, and for some moments it sounded like a police raid on a brothel, before they relapsed into harmonious snuffles.

Suspended in coops below the gallery, hens then began to cackle, but this was only a fuse leading to the grand explosion which announced the dawn. Outside each apartment was tethered a fighting cock, that is to say a cock which had attracted its owner's attention by its aggressive behaviour, its bold spirit and its defiant crowing. In the glow of the oil lamps which burned all night in the gallery, they could be seen tilting their heads from side to side as the hens continued to complain. Then one would blink and shake its wattles. It ruffled up its feathers, and then with a metallic ring it clashed its wings, threw back its head and gave forth a trumpet call to awaken the dead. Before the last notes died away, the crashing of wings announced the next deafening cry from its neighbour, and so it continued down the line, until the first bird was ready to give voice again.

It was hell, but it was worth it. For the first time we were sleeping in a longhouse which managed to appear traditional in looks as well as habits. The final decision had yet to be made but it seemed that Rumah Langga might become 'our longhouse', the paradigm for the Iban dwelling which we would construct in the minds of a million Time-Life readers.

We had passed Rumah Langga the day before on our way to check out the *gawai kenyalang* in the longhouse at the top of the Bangkit. Even from the river it looked good, but it was impossible to stop then. A furious rainstorm had broken. It blotted out the sun, and in heavy grey light the drops pinged like bullets against the river so that its surface was pitted with white eruptions. Within minutes the turquoise water was stained by mud washed off the bank, and by the time the sun came out the white

63

horsetails in the rapids had grown to smooth brown chutes. With the river high, travelling became easier, but there was another, more compelling reason for not stopping, and that was to avoid murdering each other.

Tony's unhappiness, obvious enough on the Batang Ai, turned to deep despair on the Rejang and Katibas. Not only were the clothes still wrong, but close to the ferry routes, the longhouses had invested in concrete foundations and electric light and become permanent dwellings. Resentment at Michael's interference undermined his morale, and the more irritated Michael became with his pessimism, the more depressed Tony grew. The days were ticking away, and he still did not feel he had really started. At a little town with the delightful name of Song, he had poured out his woes.

'We've been misled about these Iban,' he said drearily. 'They're really quite up-to-date. We've been travelling around with this big party of people, and there's nothing for me to photograph. What can I do with someone like Danggang in the picture?' (Danggang's sophisticated Parisian look had been complemented by a pair of snazzy sunglasses, a jockey cap marked TEXAS, and a red shirt embroidered with the slogan 'Hala Jeans – Get Into Them!') 'The whole thing's a waste of time and money,' Tony concluded, 'I'm just going through the motions.'

I might have been more sympathetic had I been less exasperated. So he had problems, what about me? How was I supposed to maintain the fiction of being a factual travel writer when our search for a longhouse to suit Time-Life's preconceptions meant that we were picking up and discarding possibilities as fast as a fashion expert examining dresses on a rail?

'Christ, you're such whingers,' Michael burst out when I complained about the hours we spent travelling. 'Tony complained all the way up the Batang Ai, now it's you. If there's any more, James and I are going to leave you both here and go straight back to Canberra.'

Even James's affable temper had become strained, and his

brown eyes took on a dangerously reddish hue, when Tony turned down as unsuitable a longhouse where some of his relatives lived. It was at that point that we reached our fragile compromise; first we would visit the top longhouse on the Bangkit, then come back downriver and, it was hoped, select a location where we could stay put. If that did not work out, we would repeat the process on the Katibas. And after that – it was hardly necessary to spell it out. The overlay of conscious moderation was vibrating from the fury below.

The peace still held as we passed Rumah Langga, but one false word would have smashed it to bits, and so we continued up the swollen river. Ading's chevroned eyes took on a more than usually anguished expression, and Ayum did not even attempt a grin, though Danggang, like the artist he was, clearly enjoyed our arguments as good raw material.

The festival was almost over when we arrived at the top longhouse, but our visit had one important consequence; coached by James, I learned about the gamesmanship of drinking *tuak*, and engaged in the first of a series of marathon drinking duels with the augurer, a burly man called Membuas. The taste of *tuak* varied from sour apples to condensed milk, but its alcoholic content was less than that of light wine. It was, however, served in half-pint glasses and pint-sized bowls, and the host's intention was to make the guests drunk before they drank him dry.

It was in James's nature to accept a challenge, even one as crude as this, not merely without a second thought but as though a new colour had been added to the rainbow. Although good manners required guests to accept the *tuak* offered, good sense required them to impose as many conditions as possible – that a *pantun* or praise-song be sung first, that the glasses be smaller, and most effective of all that the host should drink first. With James's encouragement, we made such inroads into the jar of Membuas's *tuak* that after emptying one more bowl, I exclaimed vaingloriously, 'The service is getting kind of slow around here, James, a man could die of thirst before he got a refill.' With a grin, James passed this on to the shifting group of hosts, guests

65

and praise-singers around us. Membuas was preoccupied by his duties as augurer, but his family responded by dragging out a fresh vat, and so won the contest handsomely. Membuas, however, must have decided that this was an unsatisfactory riposte, for whenever we met subsequently he wanted a re-match. This first experience of an Iban 'drunk' thus led to a marathon series of drinking bouts, the last of which gave rise to some profound conclusions about sex and death. That was in the long term; in the short, it merely delayed the moment of truth. When we embarked the next morning for the return downriver, the tension was still humming.

Rumah Langga had only twelve apartments, which made it slightly smaller than the average longhouse, but it was built on classic lines without a trace of corrugated iron or concrete. Roofed with wooden shingles, it not only looked good but, as we discovered when we trooped inside, the interior was cool. Although the day was hot there was a whisper of a breeze coming through the open doorways and windows. We watched Tony anxiously as he explored it, occasionally peering through his view-finder to check his impressions.

'Well, what do you think of it?' Michael demanded when he returned, and his voice had the unforgiving quality of a chef who had seen his previous three soufflés sent back to the kitchen.

Tony looked past him to the far end of the gallery. 'It'll do,' he said shortly. Then turning to me he asked, 'Does it suit you?'

Fearful of betraying too much enthusiasm, I said that I thought it would be fine. For their part, the two anthropologists agreed that at first glance the longhouse seemed to contain a good cross-section of Iban life. There was an almost audible easing of emotion. Even the timing seemed right, for the *gawai kenyalang* here was not due to begin for another week. If its inhabitants were prepared to accept us this would be the place. We had asked to stay the night, and now lying sleeplessly on my mat, I became impatient for the dawn, to see whether our optimism was justified.

Through the doorways and windows the black outline of palm

fronds and banana trees could be seen against the dark sky. As the light grew stronger, details of the interior appeared. The steep roof rose to its apex over a wooden wall which divided the apartments from the gallery. Jutting out over the wall was a loft which held mats, baskets and enormous bark bins containing each family's harvest of rice. The edge of the loft was supported by a row of pillars, marching down the centre of the gallery, each of which was hung with the personal belongings of a family. There were fishing-nets, harpoon-guns and outboard engines; there were rice baskets, bush-knives and rice mills; there were straw coolie hats, plastic hard-hats, felt cowboy hats and warriors' head-dresses decorated with black and white hornbill feathers; and there were nets made out of creepers which held a strange catch of grey, fibrous-looking hollow balls. Only when dawn had properly arrived did I identify them – they were skulls.

I had to put in my contact lenses to study them properly, because the idea of getting up to gaze short-sightedly into an empty eye-socket was not attractive. Twice a day during the rituals of insertion and extraction I used to give thanks that I had gone to the lens-friendly jungle instead of the Sahara. A glass of water for rinsing and two or three blinks gave me twenty-twenty vision. There were sixteen skulls altogether, one of which looked as though it was of a caveman, but they all belonged to the three central apartments in the longhouse. Although I looked at them sympathetically, mindful of the fecundity they carried, I could find nothing phallic in them. Yet as late as 1949, the *Sarawak Gazette*, the country's semi-official newspaper, had warned its readers of the erotic emotions aroused by a head. The bloody scenes at the end of the Second World War had renewed the enthusiasm for old customs, and, the paper cautioned, 'nobody who has seen the girls change into little furies of excitement when a fresh head is brought in can doubt that the grim spectre of headhunting will raise its dismembered trunk on the slight relaxation of vigilance.' A generation had passed, yet something of their magic must have remained with them. The families who did not have some grey crania hanging outside their apartments owned far fewer possessions than those who did. The seed was apparently still bearing fruit.

Soon after the first ringing cock-crow, the women had been on the move. They emerged silently from the apartments, carrying buckets and gourds to fill at the river. When they returned with water for cooking, the men started to come to life. A low conversation began further up the gallery. The smell of wood fires seeped into the air. A couple went out to check the fish-traps they had set the night before. A man urinated from the platform. Other men went down to wash at the river, and on their return brought out to the gallery the two brass boxes which every family possessed. The smaller one contained tubes of dried palm leaf and tobacco for making cigarettes; the larger held the ingredients for a betel wad – sireh leaf and tobacco leaf, an areca nut with a small grater, and a pot of lime paste. Hardly looking at what they were doing, they rolled cigarettes or made up a little parcel of leaf, nut and paste, then settled back to discuss what the night had revealed.

Up and down the long gallery, they huddled in small groups round the oil lamps, most of them squatting cocooned in their sarongs against the cool air. The yellow light gleamed on their cheek-bones and noses, and their faces had the serious concentration of punters studying form. Usually a dream only indicated the general fortune of the day. Some were bad enough to make it inadvisable to leave the safety of the longhouse, a few concerned the great turning-points in life, but most required discussion and weighing-up to extract their exact significance.

The beginning of dream analysis meant that it was time to get up. I put away my mat and cotton sleeping-bag, and having examined the skulls went to bathe. Since each family owned the section of gallery and platform outside its apartment, there were variations in the quality of wood used for the floor, and in its state of repair. In the centre of the longhouse there were planks, but the poorer families at the ends used split bamboo, and it was necessary to walk carefully with feet splayed out to avoid slipping between the slats.

Outside, the platform was on a level with the tops of the fruit trees, and between their leaves the river could be glimpsed thirty feet below. Here too you could easily tell where the wealth lay. For most of its length the platform was a springy trellis of split bamboo bound with creeper and supported on poles which were covered in ferns and moss. In the centre the bindings and poles were firm enough, but they deteriorated towards the ends so that wide gaps suddenly appeared, and some of the supports seemed to have rotted away completely. It was not as bad as one long-house on the Batang Ai where a family had walked out in a huff leaving a hole where their section of the platform used to be, but it was a useful reminder that the longhouse was a line of independent dwellings rather than a single unit.

When Iban women still wore short, knee-length skirts instead of sarongs, inquisitive boys used to stand beneath the platform and modesty compelled the women to tuck their skirts between their knees. They walked in consequence with their toes turned in – 'waddling rather than walking,' Charles Brooke remarked – and what with washing-lines strung at head height and small boys below, their journeys across the platform must have been a penance.

Two ladders led down to the bank, one from the middle of the platform, the other from the downriver end. The former at least had steps but the latter was simply a large twenty-foot log with deep notches cut into it. The heavy fall of rain had made them as slippery as grease. I descended backwards clinging to my towel and sponge-bag, and trying not to lean on the wooden rail alongside. The ladders were the only part of the building which were common property, and since no single person took responsibility for their upkeep, the creepers which tied the rails in place were not renewed when they began to rot.

At the foot of the ladder there was some level ground, where pigs rootled and cock-fights took place, and then the ground fell away to a sandy beach. The longhouse had been built on a spit of land formed by a horseshoe bend in the river, and of all those that we had inspected, it had by far the most spectacular setting.

Below the bend there were deep rapids, but upstream a long green pool widened into shallow swift-running water. On the far bank, the slope formed a bowl and at this hour a cool shadow still lay over both the pool and the longhouse. It was as close to paradise as could be imagined.

Beneath the bank, the river-bed deepened so sharply I could dive in from the shore, and the water was still cold and refreshing. I swam upstream towards a canyon of green trees which bordered the river. A dozen praus were drawn up on the beach below the longhouse, and a little further on some women were washing clothes amidst a tumble of rocks and boulders. They bent straight-legged to soap, scrub and soak, their damp sarongs clinging to their thighs and rounded haunches. It was impossible for them to look anything but attractive. The older women were supple in their movements, and with few exceptions the younger ones were slim and almost delicate. Above their sarongs, their breasts and shoulders were smooth and honey-coloured, and their long black hair was tied back in chignons to reveal high cheek-bones and neat features. I was a drifting voyeur until one of the lovely washerwomen saw me. She knotted her sarong above her breasts and said something to the others. They swung round towards me, and the sight of a pink-faced seal provoked a burst of merriment. In self-defence I let myself float away on the current.

It was one of those women, a girl of about twenty, who had sung the praise-songs the day before which had welcomed us to the longhouse. A small nose and wide mouth gave her an expression of jolly goodwill, but when she reclined on one elbow to sing, her face took on a clown-like melancholy. At first the singing sounded more Arabic than Far Eastern, a near-monotone delivered from the back of the throat and decorated with quarter-tones and rippling grace-notes. The words consisted of a bouquet of compliments, of which James offered two examples – 'great white spirit' and 'big-bellied crocodile' – before declaring that they were virtually untranslatable. I believed him. It was the girl's shining eyes, sometimes gazing past me in concentration, sometimes resting on mine, which made it an electrifying performance. I preened myself that the customary bowl of *tuak* she offered me at the end was given with a special grace. But then she sang to Ngali, and the spectacle became transfixing.

This song was like a pibroch, grace-notes multiplied to elaboration, voice heartachingly pure, and delivered with an emotion which I had not even realised was absent before. Ngali sat unmoving, his blue hat cocked over his eyes, but below the brim his set face was proud and absorbed. She sang of his courage and of his leadership of the Iban against the Japanese, and suddenly I realised what it meant to be a hero. It was not a fifteen-minute fame, but a sustained glory, recognised by gods and humans alike, that came from a life unwaveringly committed to great achievements. The praise-singer had felt it in him, and I was glad that she had celebrated it so fittingly.

The river soon carried me out of sight of the women, and pushed me to the further bank. From here the dark-brown, shingled roof of the longhouse could just be seen between the fruit trees. Behind it a steep jungle-covered slope rose to the pale, early morning sky. The longhouse and this stretch of the river were still in shadow, but now I was swirled round the corner into the brilliant rays of the rising sun. On the outside of the bend, the river had become a smooth sluice plunging towards the rapids. I swam to the shallows and, bracing my feet against a rock, let the water plummet against my back while the sun drove gleaming icicles of light between my half-closed eyes. It was a moment of pure contentment. I stayed there until growing pangs of hunger reminded me of breakfast.

The gallery was deserted when I returned, and I was about to conclude that I was too late to eat when Jingga appeared in the doorway of his apartment.

'*Makai*,' he said fiercely. '*Makai, makai!*'

Before I knew Jingga's name, I had identified him in my journal as 'Paul Scofield playing Lear'. He was admittedly shorter and fatter than Scofield, but he had the actor's resonant voice, his crisp, wavy hair and, allowing for an overlay of flesh, his chiselled

71

features. The heavy build and some greyness in the hair gave him a slow-moving dignity, and despite fleshy, sensual lips his face conveyed a tragic quality as though he were beset by secret cares.

'*Makai*' was the first word of Iban that I had learned. It meant both 'food' and 'eat', and it was impossible not to learn it because it was shouted up and down the gallery at every meal-time summoning people to eat. Like much Iban language, it sounded to my ears like a command, but Jingga also managed to suggest that it was a distraction from his deeper concerns. I smiled apologetically and went inside.

The apartment made me gulp. In the first room, where people lived, ate and slept, the floor was covered in pink linoleum, and four vinyl-covered chairs stood against the back wall. Mattresses were rolled in one corner, and a sort of wallpaper effect had been created by pinning a solid mass of magazine photographs to the wall. In the corner the row of gongs and glazed jars, which was the true measure of Jingga's wealth, seemed almost incongruous by comparison. What the purists back home would make of it was a question I preferred not to face.

It was a large room, about twenty feet square, and a short passage connected it to the kitchen which was the same width but only about twelve feet deep. At the back, where the roof sloped down to a height of a few feet, a fire burned in an open hearth beneath a rack of drying firewood. All the cooking was done here; meat was roasted on a spit over the open flames, and there was a huge iron pot for boiling rice, together with smaller aluminium pans for vegetables and a wok for frying.

The women of Jingga's family – his mother, wife, two daughters and daughter-in-law – squatted beside the hearth, and one of them, I was delighted to see, was the praise-singer. Meanwhile the men ate by themselves. Half a dozen bowls arranged in a circle contained fish, both boiled and fried, breadfruit and tapioca leaves. A large pan piled high with rice stood in the centre. Michael was already eating, so I joined him sitting cross-legged on the floor with a plate and a finger-bowl in front of me. Jingga ladled gigantic handfuls of rice on to his plate, and reproachfully regarded the small heap I put on my dish.

'*Makai!*' he commanded. I added some more, took a fish and tapioca leaves and ate.

His son, Bulik, was round and smooth with a head like a seal, and whatever his father's worries he evidently did not share them. With a broad grin he watched my clumsy effort to disentangle fish-bones from the flesh, to strip tapioca leaf from its stem and to trap the last remaining grains of rice in the bottom of my greasy plate. I had no sooner finished than he picked a particularly juicy chunk of fish from the bowl and put it in front of me. '*Makai,*' he said with a chuckle.

Not wishing to give offence, I repeated my filleting efforts with finger and thumb and ate it, leaving a mess of bones and scales behind. Bulik gestured towards the rice. '*Makai,*' he smiled.

I shook my head, and touched the bowl with my fingers to show that I meant no disrespect to its spirit.

'*Makai, makai!*' shouted the girls squatting by the hearth. I held up my hands in refusal.

'*Makai, makai, makai!*' screamed a chorus of neighbours peering in through gaps in the walls on either side.

I was about to give way beneath the overwhelming weight of public opinion, when Michael suddenly said '*Udah*', meaning 'Finished', and without further ceremony got up and left. No one seemed surprised, let alone hurt by his abrupt departure, so I followed his example though with rather less accomplishment. My legs refused to straighten after sitting on the floor, and as I hobbled out I heard the girls giggle '*Oooodaaaa*' at each other.

It was Jingga who planned to celebrate a *gawai kenyalang* and if we were to observe it, we needed his permission. Later that morning we gathered in Jingga's living-room, and for the occasion we sat in the vinyl chairs and drank Milo. As usual, the responsibility for making arrangements fell upon Michael, but with the help of his summaries, I found that I could follow the gist of the conversation by watching the flow of expression across Jingga's face.

It improved with familiarity for it revealed a succession of quite contradictory impulses. The mobile eyes and mouth that curled up into a joker's mask drooped tiredly towards despair, hardened to a peasant's appraising stare, and stretched in an urchin's grin. In the end I decided that each was genuine, and that he found the drama of an emotion irresistible.

The festival was no light undertaking. Judged purely in material terms, it would cost around $2,000 Malay; he would have to entertain twenty or thirty guests for about a week, he had to hire at least three bards to chant their sacred songs, there were offerings without number to be made, hens and pigs to be sacrificed, and up to thirty gallons of rice wine to be brewed. In the normal course of events he would not have undertaken such an expensive business, but the decision had been forced upon him. Three years ago, Langga, the headman of the longhouse, had dreamed that Jingga would hold a *gawai kenyalang*. This in itself might not have been decisive but for a detail about the ritual cock-fight which preceded the festival. If Jingga's bird won the fight, so the dream went, he would make a lot of money, far more than the cost of the festival itself. At first Jingga had been dubious, but soon he started to have the same dream, although now it seemed that the promised reward of wealth would come to him without his even having to work for it. Convinced at last, Jingga had begun preparing for his *gawai kenyalang*.

At the heart of the festival was a story. It concerned Singalang Burong, the bloodthirsty god of war and fertility, who would hunt down the souls of Jingga's enemies and bring their heads to the longhouse to be the seeds of Jingga's future good fortune. In head-hunting days, the destruction of his enemies' souls would have enabled Jingga to defeat them in real life, but nowadays the enemies were impersonal – obstacles to success rather than people. The god whose aid he was enlisting had not lost its power, however, and in acting out the story it behoved Jingga to take care so that the power should not be turned against him.

For this festival, Singalang Burong was represented not in his normal guise of a kite but by the effigy of a hornbill. Of all the

74

birds in the jungle, the Rhinoceros Hornbill is the most instantly identifiable. The first time I saw one was when I was pig-hunting with James. As I stood silently listening for oinks and grumphs, a raucous roar came from the treetops, and with a startling whoosh of wingbeats, a pheasant-sized bird with the colouring of a magpie and the face of a gargoyle clattered through the leaves on to the branch of a nearby tree. It had a long, curved ivory beak surmounted by an upward-tilted, red and yellow horn. This extravagant beak could be sold for its ivory, the flesh could be eaten, and the elegant white tail-feathers barred with a black stripe made an essential decoration for Iban headgear on ritual occasions. It was therefore a bird of plenty which explained why it represented the god on this occasion. Odder than its appearance, however, are its breeding habits. The female makes her nest in a hollow tree close to a convenient hole in the trunk, and is then walled in by her mate using a gum secreted in his stomach which hardens to cement on exposure to the air. Only the extraordinary casque is left protruding, and she remains imprisoned, relying on the male to pop pellets of food into her open beak, until after her eggs are hatched.

An effigy of the hornbill was carved out of soft, green wood in an imaginative, almost expressionist representation of the original. In the hands of an expert woodcarver, the curve of the bill was exaggerated and the tail-feathers elongated until they formed a single curlicue, balanced by the upturned casque which grew to a fantastic ornate whorl. It was brightly painted in red, green and yellow, and decorated with symbolic figures of men and animals.

Ideally Jingga should have gone to such an expert for his effigy, but he prided himself as a handyman, and undertook the work himself. My first lessons in Iban took place at the foot of his effigy, learning the names of the different figures carved on it. '*Aso*,' Jingga would say, pointing at a hunting-dog running down the bird's wing. '*Gajah*,' and his finger would rest on a tiny elephant perched on the tail. There were human forms too, representing Jingga and his family whose fortunes the rapacity of the dogs

75

and the strength of the elephant were supposed to serve. Since the Iban usually had neither the patience nor the inclination to teach basic skills – if you had not learned as a child, their attitude implied, you had best sit quietly out of the way – Jingga's lessons were a token of the generosity of his nature.

Unfortunately the carving was crudely done, and Ngali found his choice of symbols alarming. He pointed out that there were many hunting dogs running down the hornbill's back but that Jingga had omitted to provide any prey for them to catch. There was a danger that in their frustration the hunting spirits might turn upon Jingga and his family. It did not bode well.

Once the effigy had been made, it sat in a wooden box, referred to as its nest, which was placed on the beams above the gallery. When a visitor arrived, he was expected to make a contribution towards the cost of the festival in return for a praise-song and the goodwill of the effigy. Some money also came in from Jingga's son, Bulik, who was on *bejalai* working as a tractor-driver at Miri, an industrial town on the coast, and from his Chinese son-in-law who was employed in the timber yards at Bintulu on the other side of the Rejang.

Once Jingga had announced his intentions, other families began to prepare their own smaller rituals and feasts for the same time. For this they too needed quantities of surplus rice for the *tuak* and to feed their guests. Among the poorer families, especially those at the downriver end of the longhouse, there was little to spare. Their previous year's harvest had been poor, and they could hardly afford to make more than a gallon or two. By contrast, the two families in the centre, those of the headman, Langga, and the augurer, Mandau, had done excellently, and they would have no difficulty in producing fifteen or twenty gallons each for their own sumptuous celebrations.

Nevertheless, Jingga's festival was the most important of them all. Earlier in the year, invitations in the form of a bottle of *tuak* and an offering of rice and eggs had been sent to eight longhouses on the Bangkit, and in the traditional way those invited had signified acceptance by consuming the wine and presenting the offerings to the spirits. To satisfy the thirst of so many guests, Jingga would need about two hundred pounds of glutinous rice, enough to make close to thirty gallons of *tuak*. He would need another four hundred pounds of rice for all the offerings, and as much again for the food. It was no time for a bad harvest. Jingga's was a disaster.

There were reasons. He had planted early, he explained, and when the others came to burn their farmland, the ashes had fallen on his green shoots and stunted their growth. Later a landslide had carried away part of his seeded land, and much of the rest had been destroyed by pigs and monkeys. As though that were not bad enough, two hammer blows had followed. First, the bottom fell out of the pepper market so that there was hardly any profit to be earned from his farm, and then his Chinese son-in-law lost his job and was unable to send him any more cash. Another daughter whose husband might have been expected to contribute something had been abandoned and been forced to return home. The Lear-like look of suffering on Jingga's face was no pose. In the circumstances his initial response to our request to stay for the festival was magnanimous.

'You are welcome to stay,' he growled, 'but if you eat up all our rice, we'll boot you back down to the Rejang.'

It was only as Michael and he talked that the story of his setbacks emerged. With less than a week to go before the festival began, he had still not been able to buy enough eggs, chickens and arak. Tactfully Michael suggested that we might contribute some of these items. A strange expression came over Jingga's face, half-cunning, as though we might be a chance to exploit, and half-noble, as though – well, as though we might be his dream coming true.

'If you do that,' he announced with dignity, 'I shall treat you as members of my family.'

The look in our eyes was presumably no less ambiguous. Despite the plastic chairs, three of the women in his apartment were bare-breasted: at worst some photographs could be taken, and at best – we had found the family Lou had been dreaming of back in London.

During that break in the farming year, from mid-May to mid-June, when the festival season takes place, it was impossible to buy chickens and eggs from a longhouse because every family needed its own supply for sacrifices and offerings. The nearest place we could hope to find them was at Kapit, a town higher up the Rejang. It would mean travelling again but Michael's argument was persuasive.

'If we provide food for his *gawai kenyalang* we'll be able to see it from the inside,' he pointed out. 'And at Kapit we could get a calf or a deer. That would do Jingga's prestige a lot of good because they have had no luck hunting and there hasn't been any meat in the longhouse for months.'

Inspired by his vision, I took out my journal and at his dictation scrawled down a shopping-list whose items included '50 eggs, 20 bottles of arak, 10 chickens, 1 calf or deer'. In my enthusiasm, it never entered my mind to think how these would be transported in a dugout canoe. The important fact was that we were launched on a tide of good fortune. Whatever omens the editors of Time-Life had read, they must have been as auspicious as Jingga's, for the spirits were evidently expecting us at Rumah Langga.

With a few days to go before the festival began, Tony decided to have his first photographs flown back to London for Time-Life to examine. He would have to retrace our steps to Kuching and find a courier there to take them on, and Michael was dubious as to whether he had enough time. Tony was adamant. He needed to know authoritatively whether the Iban looked primitive enough, and nothing would deflect him. Since James also wished to go downriver to visit his parents, our party divided. Ngali, Limbang and Ading stayed with Michael and me when the others left.

The evening after their departure there was a dance. It was organised by the women of Jingga's apartment who brought gongs out on to the gallery and laid them on a frame so that they could be played like the gongs of a gamelan orchestra. The occasion did not really take off, but for me that did not matter because the praise-singer was behind one of the gongs and kept smiling at me from under her lashes. A press-gang of three younger girls, no more than twelve or thirteen years old, began to roam around the longhouse forcing the men to dance. There was nothing subtle about their method. They would gather round their victim, grab him by the arms, and with muscles hardened by pounding rice and poling canoes, drag him to his feet and on to the floor. A seemly show of resistance was expected, but most men were delighted by the opportunity to show off, usually in a dazzling array of kicks, swirls and punches apparently borrowed from a martial arts class. The women practised a more Hindu style, sinuously turning ankle and wrist in a gently seductive display.

By now I realised that the praise-singer did indeed have her eyes on me. She kept losing rhythm on the gongs while she flashed the sweetest smiles at me from beneath her lashes. Seeing what was happening the rest of the band began to giggle so that the music, never wonderful to begin with, hardly existed. I didn't care. In a T-shirt and sarong she looked delicious, and her smile would have melted rock. I could hardly wait for the dance gang to reach me and carry me to the floor. There I danced a Highland Fling in which I sprang more lightly, stretched the stags' antlers higher, and pointed the feet more deftly than I had done since I was ten years old and in Miss Buchanan's dancing class.

Aching was her name, pronounced as Time-Life would put it 'Ah-ching'. She came over and sat beside me after my Highland Fling, but what Miss Buchanan would have said when she laid her leg over my thigh, I hesitated to think. That sort of behaviour had never come up during her homilies on etiquette and correct deportment. I was not really capable of any rational processes at all, though I was conscious of some interchange between Michael and Jingga.

'He wanted to know if you were married,' Michael said to me. 'I told him you were.' (In fact I was not.)

Jingga leaned forward and caught my eye. His mouth was swollen by a huge wad of betel, its juice had stained his lips fire-engine red, and the whites of his eyes were streaked flame-red. He flicked a glance towards Aching and back to me, then raised a huge spatulate thumb in approval. It seemed that I would be gaining a father-in-law as well. One of the older women shouted a remark, to which Michael made an immediate retort. It was greeted by a guffaw of laughter, and at once the warm weight of Aching's thigh was lifted from mine.

'What was all that about?' I asked Michael suspiciously.

'She wanted to know whether you would take a second wife,' Michael said with a grin. 'I told her you weren't up to it.'

There is no relationship more vulnerable to abuse than that involving an interpreter. I turned to Aching to convey to her that I had been traduced, but she had already slipped inside her father's apartment. Still, I thought, there is time, we shall be coming back after our visit to Kapit, and then I shall make do without an interpreter.

At breakfast the next morning, she was subdued, but darted the occasional look over her shoulder as she squatted at the hearth. When our half of the party loaded up the prau, she came out on to the platform to wave goodbye. There was the briefest glimpse of her, and then we were round the bend in the river and bucketing down the swollen rapid.

A change of plan made while my mind was distracted by other matters included a detour on our journey to Kapit. Instead of turning right as we emerged from the tree-covered mouth of the Bangkit and proceeding down to the Rejang, we turned left. This took us up the Katibas river, first to a wealthy two-storey longhouse with a concrete floor where a spectacular *gawai ken-yalang* was coming to an end, and then, since we had time to spare, to its upper reaches to explore for places to photograph.

The catchment area of the Katibas contains some of the highest hills on the border with Kalimantan. Rain had been falling there for days, and the river was gigantic, a brown flood barrelling down the waterway with branches, trunks and tree-stumps swirling in its grip. Limbang acted as lookout, obviously relishing the challenge, and the sallow, middle-aged man who had started out with us now appeared to be getting younger with each day.

On most rivers the topmost longhouse is wealthier than others lower down because it has no competition for its fishing or for use of the jungle. This one was an exceptionally handsome building, roofed in bilian wood, and we had no hesitation in pulling in to the bank.

A crowd collected on the platform as we landed, and more joined them when we began to unload the prau. Suddenly there were shouts of alarm followed by a rending crash. I turned round in time to see a section of the platform collapse and bodies, black against the sky, tumbling fifteen feet to the ground beneath.

Limbang was the first to react, and he took off like an arrow up the bank to the longhouse. We rushed behind him to find a crowd of women and children shouting and weeping amid a tangle of splintered bamboo and broken poles. It was clear that too many people had gathered on the platform, and the supports had snapped under their weight. For a moment the noise and the sprawling bodies made it seem as though a major catastrophe had occurred, but quite quickly people began to pick themselves up nursing nothing more serious than scrapes and cuts. At last there was only one person still on the ground, an enormously fat woman who sat surrounded by smashed bamboo moaning and occasionally crying out, 'I want something to eat.'

Once the shock of alarm passed, the Iban sense of humour, which was geared towards slapstick comedy, began to reassert itself. For the benefit of late arrivals, onlookers pantomimed the struggles of the girl clinging to a pole who had simultaneously tried to keep her hold and pull her rucked-up sarong over her knees. Limbang imitated another who, he said, had been swinging like a monkey, small boys began to mock each other's terror, and soon there was more laughter than tears.

Relatives carried the fat woman to her apartment and plastered her in turmeric. I was disinfecting her torn hands while her skin was being painted yellow. The woman's left leg was numb and the base of her spine was hurting, yet the only medicine available was a sympathetic magic which imagined that the turmeric would draw off excess heat from her body. In the night her pain grew worse, and the longhouse's healer was sent for. His remedy was to cup her.

First he pricked the skin over her kidneys, then he put a spill of burning paper on the pinprick and covered it with a small glass. For a few seconds the paper continued to burn, but once the flame went out, the vacuum began to draw blood to the surface and the glass sank into the ochrous mass of the woman's flesh. When the healer pulled it off, it came free with a loud sucking noise leaving a circle of raised flesh from which blood continued to seep. The healer swabbed it clean and repeated the process on her shoulder. Throughout the ordeal, the woman lay sprawled face down on her mat, and despite her grimaces of pain, she did not complain.

It was not until I saw this remedy, which had been practised in medieval Europe to draw off an excess of humours or 'bad' blood, that the implications of living in a magical world began to dawn on me. There were no cures for pain and illness except those of sympathetic magic. Apart from those injured by the collapse of the platform, a stream of people came to us each evening with various ailments, many of which were trivial enough to be treated with our own sympathetic magic. During the festival season, for example, the acidity of *tuak* produced an epidemic of stomache ache and Michael doled out quantities of Milk of Magnesia tablets along with the vitamin pills and aspirins. For the women with sores on their legs which had spread into inflamed, pus-filled chancres or the feverish children with burning foreheads, there was nothing between them and the great fear of disablement and death except the possibility that the white spirits or the government clinic six hours downriver might invest their remedies with a power greater than the cures of their own healer. Magic trapped you in a circular world. No one could have illustrated it more clearly than Ngali.

As the shadow of catastrophe passed, he appeared to have

forgotten his doubts in the warmth of the welcome that enveloped him. He had hardly been settled on the headman's gallery when someone at the back of the crowd asked, 'Ngali is here?' From those in the front the answer was shouted back, '*Iya poh*', '*Iya poh*' – he himself. Ading was talking to a friend whom he had last met thirty-seven years before, but the moment his friend heard that Ngali had come, he got up and led the old hero away to his apartment.

'Hey,' Ading shouted, 'we've only just met after all these years, why are you going off with Ngali?'

His friend glanced over his shoulder. 'It's not every day you meet someone you thought was in heaven.'

Later that night a deaf man, who had apparently sensed the excitement but not identified the cause of it, sat down beside Ngali.

'What have you done with your life?' he asked.

'Oh a bit of farming, a bit of fishing, a bit of hunting,' Ngali replied.

The deaf man looked at him suspiciously. 'I thought there was something more than that,' he said.

'Nothing good,' Ngali answered briskly.

Cousins competed to feed him, and it would have been easy to extend our stay, but soon he became anxious to leave. There was no apparent reason for his anxiety, and it was not until we stopped to eat after putting some fifteen miles of river between us and the longhouse that he offered an explanation. On the way to the longhouse, he said, he had heard one of Singalang Burong's augury birds. In this case it was a *pangkas* or Maroon Woodpecker, and it had called from our right-hand side. Had we been on a hostile mission, it would have been an excellent omen for it signified the rout of enemies. Heard on the right, it became stronger still, and when it was combined with the victorious aura surrounding Ngali, it created a power which was almost invincible.

Months later, I was reading the *Iliad* and found a passage in which King Priam, about to ride into the midst of the Greeks to rescue Hector's body, prays for an omen of exceptional power. He asks Zeus to send an eagle, 'a bird of omen, your swift ambassador, the one that you yourself like best, the strongest thing on wing. Let it fly on the right so that I can see it with my own eyes and put my trust in it.'

In exactly the same fashion, Ngali had searched for omens in times of conflict and drawn strength from them, but amongst friends such an accumulation of force was extremely dangerous. It had certainly been the cause of the platform's collapse, and if we had stayed longer, Ngali insisted, it would surely have resulted in someone's death. One obvious potential victim was the fat woman lying on her mat, her skin bright yellow and blood welling from blisters on her kidneys and shoulder, but it was a discouraging idea that her best hope of recovery lay in our leaving.

With the throttle wide open and the muddy torrent beneath us, we reached the Rejang by early afternoon, but after that there was slow progress against the current and it was dark before we reached Kapit. The town served the whole of the hinterland of the Rejang river, where Kayan, Ukit and Kenyah people lived as well as the Iban. It too had been founded by Charles Brooke, and was equipped with a white-painted government building as well as numerous Chinese shops and a bazaar. It may have been a reaction against the primitive quality of the medicine, but I found that everything modern, the lights, the cold beers, the newspapers, had an irresistible charm.

The next morning Michael went off to buy the hens. In my mind's eye I expected him to return with plucked, naked bodies, so it came as a surprise when he returned with a dozen squawking hens.

'Well, you don't expect Jingga to sacrifice a quick-frozen, battery chicken, do you?' he demanded briskly.

Reluctantly I accepted his point, but the hens were only the thin end of the wedge. For the first time since we arrived on the Rejang, his urchin grin had returned, displacing the increasingly apparent look of fatigue.

'I've managed to find a deer,' he said. 'This will establish Jingga's reputation to be able to offer his guests venison.'

Even then my imagination failed me. I could only summon up a picture of the tragic look on Jingga's face giving way to surprise and pleasure as we presented him with a haunch of venison. There was besides hardly time to think the matter through; it was necessary to wrap up the eggs so that they did not make a giant omelette in the prau, to persuade the arak salesman that the kerosene smell of the liquor he had sold us came from petrol in the jerrycan rather than the arak's own petroleum stink, and to buy myself a batik shirt to dazzle Aching. The next morning Michael took me to a hardware shop behind the main square.

'There it is,' he said.

I should have guessed. It was no haunch of venison we were to take with us, but a soft-eyed, damp-nosed, warm-blooded, cuddly lookalike for Bambi, the pet of a Chinese family, which at that moment was contentedly grazing on the grass behind their hardware shop. Even Ading, who was in charge of the dugout, looked a little doubtful when he heard of the plan. His face cleared when Michael explained that, because I came from a country called Scotland which was filled with deer, I was an expert in handling these animals.

'Good,' said Ading with relief, 'we shall leave it to Andro.'

Whatever Michael might say, it was obvious to the inhabitants of Kapit from the moment I began dragging the poor beast across the main square that I was a novice at the business. By the time I got the deer down to the bank where the dugout was beached, the prospect of free entertainment had attracted a generous-sized crowd. I had foreseen the need to rope the deer's legs, and had prepared a noose which I neatly slipped round its front legs. I was engrossed in running the rope behind the back legs when a cheer from the crowd announced that the beast had slipped the noose as effortlessly as a magician, and in the moment it took me to discover what was happening renewed applause greeted its success in kicking the loop off its hindquarters. I tried tying the front and rear legs on one side together, and was hoicked into the dust as it lunged sideways. I lassooed the hind legs, and almost had my hand broken when it kicked back at me. For fifteen minutes it disposed of every attempt to rope it with contemptuous ease, and each of its victories brought the same shouts of delight and laughter from the crowd. It was hot enough to begin with, but the added sweat of desperation, embarrassment and exhaustion almost drowned me. At last, more from despair than design, I caught hold of a hind leg, the deer lashed out, overbalanced, and as it fell I hurled myself on top of it like a wrestler. This triumph of Scottish deer-roping gave Ading time to tie up both sets of legs, and at last the deer lay still.

Once the battle was over and the adrenalin had ebbed, I began to feel profoundly miserable and the journey back to the Bangkit was nightmarish. The deer lay at the bottom of the prau, tightly trussed by Ading, and every few minutes gave out a long, piteous howl of agony. As though in sympathy, the rain pelted down and a cold wind blew, and the hours on the river crawled by, accompanied by useless, stabbing remorse. I was not merely a participant in a murder, I was a torturer too.

The arrival of our floating farmyard did bring a momentary relief to Jingga's careworn face, and once the deer had been tethered beside the longhouse, the hens cooped beneath the floor, and the eggs and arak piled in the living-room, he declared that we could indeed regard ourselves as members of his family. It was undoubtedly a touching moment, but alas I missed it. Nor did I see Aching's look of admiration as Ading told her how I had captured the deer.

By the sort of bad luck that makes a man question the auguries, Jingga decided to bring forward the date of his *gawai kenyalang* by two days. We had reached the Bangkit on our way back from Kapit when we heard the news at a poor, darkened longhouse where the coming of night had forced us to stay. It meant that Tony had to be summoned back from Kuching immediately. A telegram could be sent from Song, but unless he started at once, he would be too late for the ritual cock-fight with which the festival began, and every moment of delay he would miss more.

86

Having warned him about the uncertainty of the dates, Michael was all for letting him stew.

'He'll just have to miss it then,' he exclaimed. 'It's typical of him. He didn't listen when I told him about covering up in the sun, and he got crippled by sunburn. He didn't listen when I told him about the dates, and now he's in Kuching instead of being here. He's hopeless.'

Privately I agreed. This was unfair because I knew Tony had been instructed to send back an early sample of photographs as soon as possible. But for me another consideration loomed larger. If Tony failed to shoot Jingga's festival, our travelling, our quarrelling and deer-murdering would all have gone for naught. No matter how many clean-nostrilled chiefs he shot in noble pose, regardless of the breasts he caught naked of Western encroachment, Lou would not forgive the loss of the hornbill festival. It constituted a picture essay, the key episode in a product of exact specifications. The marketing had been done, the suburban auguries consulted from Düsseldorf to Valencia, and every detail of our conduct had to be guided by their findings or the gods of Time and Life would turn against us.

'I'll have to go back to Song,' I concluded.

5

Primitive Emotions

I LEFT EARLY the next morning while the air was still fresh. It made the deer shiver in its wooden enclosure by the steps down to the river, and it puckered the long, vertical scar on the boatman's belly. The wound had been left, he said, after an operation to remove ratshit which an enemy had put in food during a festival. My own limited experience of festivals suggested the alternative diagnosis of a stomach ulcer inflamed by the acidic action of *tuak*, though rage at absent photographers might have produced the same burning sensation.

The water flowed fast and clear, and the Bangkit was too beautiful not to be soothing. At first the steep hills and over-hanging trees created a green trough, but later in the morning the land grew flatter and a string of extravagantly curling clouds appeared above the treetop-scalloped horizon. We stopped for a smoke beside an enormous tree with saffron leaves which stood alone in a clearing, and as I stepped ashore my clothes were covered in butterflies. My shirt and trousers had not been washed for days, and a fluttering suit of indigo, crimson and yellow wings probed at every sweaty fibre. At each armpit and between my legs there was an extra ruff of colour – never was body odour more exotically represented – and when I ran shouting with pleasure, my passage was marked by a stream of butterfly bunting.

Guilt at my enjoyment impelled me to marshal a list of arguments to justify being there. To be a love object for lepidoptera with low tastes would have been enough for me but not, I felt, for Time-Life. I needed to show them that the upriver Iban were indeed wild, not perhaps in terms of being naked from the waist up, but by Levy Brühl's definition of living in a unitary world.

It was true that back in the prau an outboard engine roared into life to drive us downriver, that only the older women in the longhouse habitually went bare-breasted, that there were probably as many chain-saws hanging from the central pillars as adzes, that Mandau, the augurer, undeniably possessed a petrol-driven generator, and that at the mouth of the Bangkit, where it flowed into the Katibas, there was indeed a cluster of white government buildings which included a school and a medical clinic.

The difficulty was that this evidence for the encroachment of the modern world was all too visible, while the evidence against came in word and thought. The *tuai burong* or augurer was a case in point. Everything I had read about his responsibility for consulting the omens, reading the auguries, and interpreting dreams, had conjured up a picture of someone rather like a witch doctor or shaman. At Rumah Langga, the augurer had the precise manner of an accountant.

Mandau was in his late fifties, a handsome, neat-featured man with thick grey hair cut boyishly round a small head. There was not an ounce of surplus flesh on his spare body, and his dedication to work kept him as fit as an athlete. In his apartment were many jars and gongs, and at the back of it stood the petrol-driven generator which on important occasions lit fluorescent lights in the living-room and on his section of the gallery. No one else could offer such conspicuous evidence of material wealth. Yet all this he owed to dreams.

'Without dreams', he said firmly, 'you can do so much, you can stay alive but you will not grow rich. With the sanction of dreams you can achieve great things, with the right dreams there is no limit to what you can do.'

His achievements were precisely why the community had

89

appointed him augurer. Since it was impossible to be successful materially without a close understanding of the spiritual world, it followed that the wealthiest person had the greatest spiritual knowledge. And so paradoxically Mandau, who owned the most modern technology, the latest outboard and chain-saw as well as the generator, was by a long chalk the most traditionally minded member of the longhouse.

Yet even he did not present a greater contrast between outer appearance and inner reality than Danggang. The bard's outrageous cap and dark glasses might drive Tony to distraction, but in a society without writing he was a genius.

His astonishing power had become clear on our first journey up the Bangkit soon after Ngali's emotional reunion with his sister. Darkness was falling when we found a half-built longhouse, and although the families were too poor to feed us they welcomed us to stay for the night. It had been a long day, and I was ready to sleep, but as we sat restfully in the warm darkness after supper, James decided to bring the evening to life. Casually he remarked to our hosts that Danggang was a bard of some skill.

It was as though Bogart fans had been told that *Casablanca* was being shown on television. The entire adult population of the longhouse at once clustered round, grey-haired men – one with a head-hunter's tattoos – toothless old women, young men and girls. Two forceful middle-aged women pushed the rest of us out of the way so that Danggang could sit in the middle of the platform. Then everyone sat back and waited for him to begin. But the television would not work. Danggang said he was tired. The two ladies brought him some cushions to make him more comfortable. Danggang complained that he could only recite lying down. They brought him a sleeping-mat and a blanket. He said that he had a headache. They massaged him. Still he would not recite. They wheedled and they shouted. They caressed him and shook him, but his sharp features only grew more despondent, and his nasal voice more plaintive.

'I don't know any songs,' he said. 'I'm tired, let me go to sleep.'

Infuriated, they pulled away his blanket. They threw themselves on top of him, tickled him, pinched him and tried to pull off his sarong.

'How can I sing', he protested, 'when I've been punched and sat on?'

His protests were useless. For two hours the women did not cease to shake him and shout at him, and for good measure they shook and shouted at us whenever we tried to sleep. Finally, at one o'clock in the morning, Danggang made a concession.

'All right,' he said. 'I'll recite, but on one condition, you must sing first.'

This caused consternation, and the twenty-odd faces looked at each other to see who would begin. Eventually the noisier of the two women leant forward, propping her weight on one arm, and sang in a low throaty voice. She was followed by her fellow-tormentor, and then came a good-looking young girl in a red shirt. Her voice was transfixing, and the tripping grace-notes were sobbed from her throat with purity and precision. When she had finished Danggang sat bolt upright.

'If you continue to learn,' he declared, 'your voice will become famous far beyond the Bangkit and the Katibas.'

He seemed rejuvenated. His words were no longer whined, but came out confidently and with feeling. He called peremptorily for a cushion and a glass of water, and the two termagants leapt to carry out his commands. He cracked a joke, and everyone laughed. There was normally a cheeky quality in Danggang's manner, but now he gave off the electric self-confidence of a star performer.

The epic that he told was roughly akin to the story of Odysseus making his way back home after the Trojan Wars. As Homer, or the Homeric poets, doubtless did six thousand years ago, Danggang took a well-known story and tailored it to his audience. Though the plot was set and certain passages so famous that they had to be repeated in full, the bard was expected to give his own version of other episodes. If he were skilled and his invention fruitful, his version would be remembered by

91

singers in the audience who would incorporate it when they came to tell the story in their turn. It was not inconceivable that one day Danggang's version would be copied down, and centuries later Iban scholars would debate whether he was one man or several. If his contributions survive, their distinguishing mark will be a vein of bawdy.

At the point where the Odysseus of the story meets Dido, she invites the hero into her house to take a refreshing drink, 'and feel my tits as well,' added Danggang.

'Hey, that's not right,' protested the girl in the red shirt.

Later he told how Odysseus had travelled from Sibu to Kapit, a distance of about one hundred miles, in less than an hour. 'Impossible,' exclaimed the girl in the red shirt.

'And he went faster than an Apollo rocket,' Danggang added without pause.

Her squawk of outrage was drowned in a burst of appreciative laughter. Gradually a new character appeared in the story, a saucy girl, a girl who wanted to go to bed with the hero, a girl who wore a red shirt.

'Oh, that's not fair,' wailed the one in the audience.

Coldly the hero resists all her attempts at seduction. He will not go to bed with her, he says, 'because you have a very loud voice.'

'It's not true,' shrieked the original in a very loud voice.

'And your face is covered with make-up.'

With a yelp of dismay she buried her face in her hands, and did not look up until Odysseus was again on his way back to his longhouse. At the end of the two-hour story, there was a cathartic sigh, as though they had all been far away. The two ladies patted Danggang's cushion and smoothed out his blanket with the reverence that people give to objects of great value.

We arrived at Song in the afternoon, and from the post office I sent an urgent telegram to Tony, then settled down to wait. The village was built along the river bank at the junction of the Katibas and the Rejang, its red dirt streets bordered by corrugated iron shops selling dried fish and gaudy clothes. I played chess with the secretary of the Chinese Chamber of Commerce who gave me a bed for the night, discussed religion with an Iban catechist called Joseph, and wrote vituperatively in my journal of Tony's failure to appear.

The more I wrote, the more impatient I became to return to Rumah Langga. It was manifestly the most suitable place to be. This was not so much a matter of personal prejudice – my hopes of Aching had been badly shaken by Michael's revelation that she had subsequently asked him to sleep with her – as the conviction that the coincidence of our aims and Jingga's dreams was too neat to be ignored. Besides I found his histrionic character beguiling.

Even a rambling account of a drunken journey upriver in the middle of the night was turned into impromptu theatre by his dramatic pauses, dying cadences and eloquent gestures. His arm wriggled like a fish to demonstrate how crooked was the course he steered; his hands gripped his thigh to indicate the size of the branches he narrowly missed; his bloodshot eye rolled histrionically upwards to show his exhausted relief at arriving home safely, and his jowls drooped with the weight of centuries as he concluded sadly, 'I used to be able to drink and steer a boat at full speed, but now, even when I'm sober, I can hardly control a big engine.'

To appreciate his skill, I had to rely on Michael or James to translate, and without their help I should have been deaf. But my own halting attempts to string sentences together gave an inkling of the sort of obstacles he had to overcome. There were no conditionals or subjunctives, in fact the only tense was the present indicative. The future was formed by adding *ka* –'want' – to the verb, and the past by adding *udah* – 'finished'. Thus it was possible to say 'You eat', 'You will (want to) eat' or 'You ate (finished eat)', but there was no possibility of saying 'Would you care to eat a little more?' Instead Jingga would glare at the plate of rice which had once more betrayed my sparrow's appetite and exclaim, '*Makai lubah*' – 'Eat slowly', meaning for a long time, which in turn meant eat a lot.

To compensate, his talk was studded with similes, and his explanations had to meander round a succession of metaphors and allusions. Thus, paradoxically, the limitations of the language placed a premium on the art of rhetoric, and Jingga was a master, as he soon proved at a meeting held to resolve a family problem which had upset the entire longhouse.

His brother, Sibat, had asked the longhouse for help in deciding what to do about the marriage of his son Lagok, and after supper all the men assembled in Sibat's living-room to discuss the problem. While they sat down in a circle, a small group of women led by Mangan, the augurer's wife, came in to give moral support to Lagok's wife. She was from another longhouse, and the difficulty arose from her sense of being an outsider. At marriage a couple could decide to live either at the wife's longhouse which was the normal practice, or at the husband's. As a rule, the outsider then became a full member of the respective parents-in-law's family. On this occasion the wife had initially been unwilling to move, and her feeling of alienation had at last prompted Lagok to demand whether she really had accepted Rumah Langga as home. It was a question posed as much to the community as to the wife. What the meeting had to decide was whether they were prepared to accept her as one of them. If they rejected her, it was likely that she would be divorced.

In a quiet conversational voice, the headman outlined the background, and then asked for further information on the state of the marriage. As others chipped in, it gradually emerged that the family was short of rice and of money to buy more, and that the strain of their situation had been exacerbated by unkind gossip overheard by the wife.

During the discussion, the girl sat desolate in the corner. When asked whether she had really accepted the longhouse as home, she answered defiantly, 'Yes, I have, on condition that when we have children, my husband looks after them properly.' Despite this, sentiment was not in her favour. Only Sibat and the women were clearly for her, while the families from the poorer ends of the longhouse were definitely against her, perhaps because she so evidently hated the poverty which was their lot. The conflicting sentiment was reflected in the headman's attitude. He sat silent after she had spoken, obviously weighing what had been said but not wholly convinced by the girl's answer.

All this time Jingga had lain slumped against a pillar. His eyes were closed, his vast belly rose and fell slightly with each slow breath, and apart from an occasional jiggle of the jaw as he shifted betel, he might have been asleep. It was only when the others had talked themselves out that he made his contribution.

'At least you can say this for the girl,' he eventually interjected. 'She isn't a Kayan and she isn't white.' There was a ripple of laughter. Laboriously Jingga sat himself upright. It took some effort, and by the time he was comfortable all attention was focused on him.

Partners were like arak, he observed conversationally, good, bad and indifferent, but marriages were after all supposed to last and they should not be broken up without good reason. The girl had done no wrong, on the contrary she had been a good influence in the apartment. Of course they were suffering from shortages, what young couple didn't? Of course there was gossip, when wasn't there gossip? The important point was that the girl had a good influence on the apartment. Everyone had heard her say that she really had moved here, and because of the effect she had on the family, her claim should be accepted.

When he had finished the mood of the meeting had undergone a sea-change. She was no longer an outsider, but someone with the same problems as everyone else. The headman's formal announcement that she had definitely moved to the longhouse voiced what they all felt, and with that the meeting broke up. Whatever other qualities Jingga might have, I was sure from the start that dullness was not one of them. Someone so given to eloquence would be bound to provide a notable *gawai kenyalang*.

It took two days to get Tony back to the longhouse, but he arrived there transformed. His beard was trimmed, his face freed of the gaunt look he had worn since London, and confidence brimmed from him. In no time he had cranked up Michael's exasperation to record new levels. Not only was he unrepentant about missing the first day of the festival, he managed to cast doubt on Michael's motives for visiting the bright lights of Kapit.

'I am a straightforward person,' he said, 'and I can't understand why you went to so much trouble to get food for Jingga. Why didn't you just give him money? It all sounds very devious to me.'

On the other hand, he did bring a new zest to his work, and within minutes of arriving back at Rumah Langga, he had begun to photograph the carousel of festivity. Michael, by contrast, looked even more drawn and strained than when I had last seen him. Had he been anyone else, I should have suggested that he take to his bed, but seeing his look of fixed determination the advice died before it reached my lips. Instead he sat down to tell me in detail of the ritual cock-fight, which had so much bearing on Jingga's future wealth.

Jingga's bird was a splendid white creature with black tail and wingtips, and the fight had taken place just after dawn on the day before we arrived. The timing was a shrewd move, for a light-coloured bird was known to fight best in the daytime, while its opponent was Langga's bronze- and black-feathered cock, and dark-coloured birds did not reach their peak until evening. Jingga had dressed himself ceremonially in a dark blue loin-cloth and a white straw hat decorated with hornbill feathers. The birds were placed in the centre of a circle of spectators, where they glared at each other, then fluttered up in the air, struck and missed. Again they faced up, lowered heads weaving from side to side. This time Jingga's champion was first in the air, slashing at the dark cock which slanted back so that the other passed over its shoulder. At once Jingga ran forward to gather up his bird and claim the victory. In other circumstances a more decisive verdict would have been expected, but Jingga was taking no chances and Langga had no wish to argue the point. Whether the gods thought the same remained to be seen. As events turned out, it seemed that Michael had been chosen to deliver their verdict.

Since our departure, the longhouse had filled up with new

faces, young men who had returned from *bejalai*, others who had been out hunting when we first arrived, and neighbours and relatives who had come from other longhouses to give a hand. In front of most doors, families and newcomers were already gathered round a jar of wine, but on Jingga's section of the gallery, the atmosphere was still tense with preparations. Old men and children were peeling pale green bamboo fronds into strips to make decorative, trailing bouquets. Lengths of bark were being woven into baskets to hold the offerings. Long bamboo poles, on which the offerings would be hoisted towards the heavens, were being split open and splayed out at one end to hold the baskets. In the living-room, saucers were laid out in rows in readiness for the offerings. The kitchen was alight with fire, silhouetted with squatting cooks, and shrouded with smoke and steam. Out on the platform, a young man with a bush-knife and a host of advisers was hacking a slot in the top of a thirty-foot tree trunk on which the hornbill effigy would eventually be perched.

Half a dozen young pigs, which had been lying pinioned on the gallery, were taken down to the river where they were washed then tied up in sacks to keep them clean. Lying in the shade of some palm-leafed shelters with only their pink and black snouts peeking through the mouths of the sacks, the pigs kicked and squealed furiously as the moment of their sacrifice approached. Inside the longhouse fighting cocks crowed incessantly, dogs howled whenever stick-wielding children found them near the mats which had been laid out for guests, and a woman called her hens to be fed with the soprano 'Hoo-hoo' of a hunting owl. Indifferent to the uproar, the hornbill effigy stood on a pedestal in the gallery, draped with flags and paper flowers, a Rothman's cigarette protruding at a jaunty angle from the side of its beak.

Bulik draped a woven blanket across the beams on the gallery to make an awning outside the apartment. Sometime during the afternoon a small murder was done behind the longhouse, and a little later dismembered parts of the gentle deer I had wrestled to the ground were distributed round the apartments. And as evening approached, the roar of outboards coming upriver announced the arrival of the last of the guests.

Two of them carried the headmen of longhouses lower down the Bangkit who were to act as warriors in the *gawai kenyalang* and fight against the spirits of Jingga's enemies. It was an honourable role since the forces which might oppose the hornbill were powerful, and so Jingga needed men of comparable strength to withstand them. There were to be five in all, and as well as the headmen he had invited two grizzled former soldiers. That left one place unfilled.

It had not escaped me that since my return Aching had shown considerably less enthusiasm for me. So far as the stress of preparations left her time for sweet smiles, I saw with the green eye of jealousy that they were now directed at Michael. Jingga who had once so approved of me had also switched affections. He now took Michael to his apartment for confabulation, and addressed him familiarly as *wai*, roughly equivalent to 'chum'. But the final evidence of his favour came just before the festival began. It was Tony who broke the news.

'That bastard Michael is going to sabotage all my shots of the festival,' he exclaimed furiously. 'Jingga's asked him to take some official part in the proceedings, and he's agreed. That means I'm going to have his white, cod's belly body appearing in every single one of my shots.'

6

Jingga's *Gawai Kenyalang*

THE CURIOUS THING about Jingga was that although his hair was grey and he walked with a weighty, aldermanic tread, he could not disguise the impression that a mischievous child lurked beneath the trappings of middle age. He was easily bored by the sort of grinding work that Mandau the augurer enjoyed. He was inclined to joke about matters which Langga the headman took seriously, and for a man in his fifties it was doubtful whether he should have enjoyed dancing as much as he obviously did.

It was just possible to infer from Mandau's remarks that the misfortunes on Jingga's farm might have been avoided with a little more effort. 'A good dream does not bring in the harvest,' he would say, quoting an Iban truism, and more than once he remarked upon the long hours he himself had invested in guarding his growing rice from pests – both insects and animals – and the rewards he had reaped thereby compared to his less fortunate neighbours.

Perhaps it was the feeling that Jingga should settle down and apply himself more seriously to the business of farming that gave rise to Langga's dream about the *gawai kenyalang*. The festival was the undertaking of a mature man, and although Jingga might not qualify initially, the preparations necessary for its success would surely induce a proper sense of discipline, quite apart from the consequences which could be expected to flow from the hornbill's triumphant journey. If that was the motive, the scheme went off at half-cock. Not only were there the financial disasters beforehand but now, on the eve of the festival, it was becoming clear that Jingga's hopes of wealth were centred not on hard work but on the acquisition of a rich son-in-law.

As one fluent in Iban, conversant with longhouse custom, and capable of presenting him with a boatload of magnificent gifts for the feast, Michael made an admirable choice. His existing family in Australia was no impediment. What Jingga wanted was someone who would support both Aching and her son, Sulang, from her previous marriage.

'If you had an Iban wife as well as your wife in Australia,' he pointed out carefully, 'you would not have to live here, you could send her money while you were in Australia.'

It went without saying that when needed Jingga's son-in-law would also provide financial assistance for him and the rest of the family. As an inducement, he offered Michael the greatest honour which was his to bestow – the role of warrior in his *gawai kenyalang*.

'I refused when he first suggested it,' Michael explained later. 'I told him I wasn't feeling well, and that it would cause problems with the photographs, but he was clearly hurt. Then he began to make difficulties about us being there so I had no choice.'

Jingga's selection made the other warriors look serious. It was not a light matter they were engaged upon. They had all previously assisted at smaller festivals, building up their own spiritual resistance until they could withstand the forces at play in a hornbill festival. In addition, each of them carried protective charms whose power might harm someone without defences or experience. Had Michael been an Iban, they would have had no doubts that the dangers were too great, but it was just possible that a white spirit could look after himself. Doubtfully they accepted Jingga's decision.

At the tip of the hornbill effigy's beak, a thin bit of wood still joined the upper and lower mandibles. With the festival about to begin, the hornbill had to be able to eat the offerings which would be made to it, and so now the beak was sawn open. The first of many cocks and hens had its throat cut and its blood drained into a bowl of wine to make a cocktail which Jingga carefully poured over the hornbill's beak. Then he picked up the effigy and with a rhythmic bass roar of 'Hoo-ha, Hoo-ha', he paraded it up the platform and down the gallery. Behind him came two attendants, dressed like him in loincloth and feathered hat. At every doorstep they stopped so that each family could pour a libation over the carved beak. Once the hornbill had been fed, it was only necessary to settle the wages of the *lemembang* or bards for the festival to begin.

At the heart of all the rituals which were to follow was the *timang* or sacred chant sung by the bards. In it they would describe the epic journey undertaken by two messengers who have been sent to take a message to Singalang Burong inviting him to the *gawai kenyalang*. When he receives the invitation, the god summons his son-in-law to help him kill the enemies of the celebrant; then carrying the heads they travel from heaven down to the longhouse, meeting many adventures along the way. At the longhouse the heads are split open and the seed which spills out is planted by Singalang Burong and his company before they return to heaven. It is epic poetry in the purest sense of the word. Its subject matter is the action of gods and heroes; to tell it in its complete form requires five days and nights of ceaseless chanting.

To commit such a work to memory is a remarkable feat, but in addition to the song appropriate to the hornbill festival, there are three others for different rites, and until he has learned all four, a bard cannot consider himself fully qualified. It is an arduous calling, which begins in childhood when the neophyte joins the chorus which accompanies the bard as he chants, repeating the words of the epic line by line. A brief period of instruction under the care of a master then precedes the years of study needed to commit the epics to memory. Understandably many content themselves with learning only two or three, and the less elaborate versions at that. Nevertheless, even at its simplest, the bard's is no small gift and he is worthy of his hire, especially since he alone cannot participate in the flow of *tuak* at a festival.

Quite what his hire should be took almost two hours of delicate negotiation at a crowded longhouse meeting. Since all the richer families were celebrating festivals which required ritual chants, there were to be four or five bards, each with a chorus of two assistants, and the rate for the hornbill festival would affect all the others. The first step was to find out what limitations there might be to their recitation. One bard explained that at a cock-fight that afternoon he had helped to fasten on the spurs, and that this might give an inappropriate sharpness to his chanting: did anyone object? No one objected. Another pointed out that he did not chant the most elaborate version: was that all right? It was. Jingga then cleared his throat and asked the most senior bard how large a reward he wanted. The old man refused to commit himself, saying that he did not know what his colleagues might want.

'How much are you getting?' Jingga asked a bard who was to chant for a rice festival.

The man demurred. 'I'm doing it for my brother,' he said. 'I would be ashamed to ask for a reward.'

Another deflected the question by saying that he was chanting at his own festival.

'Then how much are you paying yourself?' Jingga shot back, and won himself a laugh from the crowd.

Eventually the senior bard was prodded into suggesting a figure. For a *gawai kenyalang* he thought a fee of $17 Malay would be appropriate. Jingga turned to other matters, touching particularly on the prevalence of pigs in the rice fields. In short, the bard's price was too high. After a good deal of allusive talk, they finally agreed on $15 instead, and everyone was satisfied.

The next morning Bulik took one of the little pigs out of its sack and stretched it out on the platform at the head of the ladder. Then up the ladder came the five warriors who were to defend Jingga's spirit in the days ahead. With their arrival, the great event which had been three long years in the making finally started.

The leader of the warriors was a lean, wrinkled old man, clad in a loincloth, a surcoat made from the fur of a honey bear, and a hat bedecked in hornbill feathers. He held the point of his spear a few inches above the sacrificial pig's throat, then thrust downwards. It was an ineffectual blow, and the agonised squealing did not bubble into silence until Bulik drew a knife across the animal's throat. Almost at once a cock was waved over the old warrior's head, and Bulik's beautiful wife, Orin, pressed a glass of rice wine upon him.

In some cultures it may be polite for a guest to conceal his opinion of the host's liquor, but not amongst the Iban. As though he had bitten on a lemon, the warrior's lips puckered, his cheeks went hollow, his eyes clenched tight shut, and his eyebrows scrunched up like caterpillars. Then he cast an anguished look at the line of girls behind Orin. Each was dressed like her in a short woven skirt, a salmon-pink blouse, and a bodice of clinking, silver coins, and each one held a jug and a glass of the same sour liquid.

Having endured that ordeal, the warriors made an offering, the first of some thirty occasions on which the ceremony was to be performed in the next few days. Before each man were arranged the by now familiar three rows of plates containing puffed rice, glutinous rice and rice cakes. Deliberately, row by row, they transferred the ingredients to a bowl, pressed seven eggs into the rice in a circle, decorated them with tobacco and betel leaf, and planted a tiny cup of *tuak* in the centre.

Crouching just beyond the offering Tony attempted to photograph the line of intense faces without including Michael's pale skin. He was working with absolute professionalism, and only someone who had heard his outburst could have guessed at the fury beneath his concentrated expression. In fact Michael's face was more than routinely pale; his pallor was deathly and covered with a glaze of sweat, and beneath his glasses his eyes had sunk into dark sockets. The excuse about not feeling well had not been false. Other than the main actors, the scene seemed to attract little attention. The crowd talked and laughed among themselves, and continued to hit the dogs as heartily as on any other occasion. Only when Bulik produced a cock for the senior warrior's prayer did the talk die away.

A growled bellow of '*Howa – Howa – Howa*' summoned the gods to hear a prayer which called unceasingly for increase – increase of rice, of land, of family, of wealth. Sometimes the prayer talked of the challenges which the family faced and sometimes of the deeds they had accomplished. Often the gods were reminded of the richness of the feast they were being offered, but sooner or later the same words always emerged, '*Bolleh padi, bolleh duit, bolleh ringgit*' – 'Give us rice, give us wealth, give us cash.'

With a swirl of the cock, the prayer was spread across warriors and spectators like incense wafted from a censor, and the bird was passed to the next warrior who growled in his turn for the essentials of rice and wealth. Then the cock was sacrificed. Those who wished a special blessing were dabbed with its blood, and one of its feathers was planted in the offering bowl.

At the end when Bulik darted forward with a pint bowl of *tuak* for the celebrants to drink, Michael declined his share. During the ceremony he had been swaying from side to side and looked ready to faint. Now, having made the offering, he staggered away to collapse in Jingga's living-room. His forehead was burning hot, and he had a hard, dry cough. He was running a temperature of 105°, and must have found coherent thought difficult, but with iron determination he diagnosed himself as suffering from either malaria or some pulmonary infection, and ordered us to feed him anti-malaria tablets and antibiotics. His colleagues had their own diagnosis. As they had feared from the start, his spirit was being crushed by the power of their charms. So while Tony and I dosed him on pills, they dipped their charms of pebbles, rings and petrified wood in oil and rubbed them on his lips and belly in an attempt to revive his weakly spirit.

Throughout that night and the following day he remained ill.

From time to time he was fiercely alert, but for much of the period he drifted vaguely in and out of consciousness. Yet forty-eight hours later, either Western drugs or the warriors' charms or his own will-power produced an extraordinary change, for his temperature returned to normal and he was on his feet again. Long before then the news had spread up and down the Bangkit that the white spirit had succumbed to the power of the Iban spirits. When other details of Jingga's hornbill festival have faded, that lesson will still be remembered.

'I never really believed in the power of the spirits until then,' a young man said later to James Masing. He had been to school and the traditional beliefs of the longhouse had begun to appear as superstitions. 'Now', he declared triumphantly, 'I know that it is true – they do have power.'

While Michael lay sweating and half-conscious in Jingga's apartment, the other warriors built a shrine round the central pillar on his gallery from a frame of bamboo covered by a ceremonial blanket. Inside it they placed the essential tools of the rice farmer – the sacred seed and whetstones, a bush-knife, and a trough for husking rice – and the three most prized possessions of the family, a brass tobacco box, a gong and a jar. Over the shrine they hung a gourd containing some seeds of rice, nuts and fruit, and an empty grinning skull. This, the Iban's ultimate fertility symbol, represented 'the seed of the shrine', the principle of increase for which all Jingga's men had prayed. And between the shrine and the apartment door a length of red thread was tied which represented the obstacles which lay between him and their prayers' fulfilment.

Parades now seemed to follow each other without cease. Many of the activities on Jingga's stretch of the gallery were repeated for the festivities which Mandau the augurer and Langga the headman were celebrating, and to a lesser extent by every other family. A cacophony of gongs and drums signalled the appearance of the girls and young women, brightly dressed in beaded dresses, jingling coins and tall, glittering head-dresses. They were led by a bard carrying his stave of office who danced along

105

flicking his elbows and heels, and at their rear marched Jingga shouldering a flag and dragging a piglet in a basket. As they came back down the platform, the girls scattered rice over the sacrificial pigs to distract any evil spirits. Almost at once the warriors donned their finery and strapped long fighting swords to their waists. By a superhuman act of will, Michael staggered from his sickbed to join them, but this time his colleagues were taking no chances. They buckled a short bush-knife round him so that the spirits would not be further annoyed by his temerity.

The warriors' parade began bravely. The leader approached the shrine holding a naked sword in one hand, a hen and a bamboo leaf bouquet in the other. To symbolise how the obstacles to Jingga's success would be cut away, he slashed through the red thread between the shrine and the apartment, and to show how the difficulties would be swept away he whisked the bamboo leaves across the floor. Tense and half-crouched, he moved with a dancing, boxer's shuffle round the shrine then sprang at it, as though on an enemy, and with a whoop of triumph slashed the air inches from the basket. It was a dramatic performance, and the evil spirits threatening the increase which was about to come to Jingga fell away, cut to ribbons.

After the warriors had decimated the forces hostile to him, they removed their surcoats and swords and passed them on to the other male guests. These too showed a determined face in their slaughter of Jingga's enemies, but their successors were younger and more self-conscious. What had been high drama quickly deteriorated to the standard of amateur theatricals. While the old men had been serious, the young moved clumsily and the war-whoop reduced them to nervous giggles. Unable to bear the sight of Bulik shuffling round the shrine wearing bathing trunks and smoking a cigarette, I turned to watch the ceremony on Mandau's part of the gallery. The contrast was illuminating. Here even the youths circled, whooped and stabbed with savage concentration. Their loincloths were knotted more flamboyantly, their sword scabbards were more ornate, and their surcoats seemed more furry. A horrid suspicion about Jingga's surcoats now hardened to certainty. Mandau's men wore the skins of honey bears on their backs, as had the most senior of Jingga's men. But the rest of his warriors – I looked again – yes, Jingga's warriors were quite clearly wearing deep-pile nylon rugs.

That was almost my last coherent thought, for offerings were being made in all parts of the gallery, and the *tuak* which followed flowed in spate. Without warning the bards began their incantations. In teams of three they strolled up and down the gallery, the leader striking the floor rhythmically with a long staff which had a clapper on the end. Their nasal drone, which was to continue for several days and nights, was at first strange, then irritating and finally hypnotic.

The fierce, familiar cry of '*Makai, makai*' woke me from a bardic trance, and I found that the gallery outside the central three apartments of Jingga, Mandau and Langga had become a dining-room. Twenty or thirty yards of floor were covered with plates of venison (I knew exactly where from), boiled hen, bamboo shoots, breadfruit, fish – boiled, broiled and baked – and rice in every form. It was the sort of banquet which in Europe went out of fashion in the seventeenth century, a potlatch feast indicating the host's readiness to break himself in order to satisfy his guests' appetites.

I ate with Langga's guests, and we did nobly I think, forging like ice-breakers through a sea of snow-white *tuak*. Our speeches were rich in prayers for the increase of Langga's wealth and rice, but when we sank back to the ground it was to find that the object of our prayers had repaid us by requiring us to drink not a bowl of *tuak* but a tumbler of brandy. Sometime later I can remember a girl singing me a praise-song, and her features behaved like a kaleidoscope. Her ears multiplied round the rim of her face, her mouth split into a dozen different orifices, and a necklace of eyes circled her nose which swelled and shrank with each note of her song.

The squeal of a pig being slaughtered awoke me. It came from the platform, an indignant cry which ended in a bubbling grunt. The sun had not yet appeared and a grey mist hung over the hilltops, but the platform had already been draped with blankets so that one section was divided off from another. There were five pigs on Jingga's section, and their deaths came quickly. A long-handled knife resembling a cut-throat razor was drawn across the throat, and as the pig gave its dying kick a deep incision opened the belly from ribs to groin. A twist of the body emptied out the hot entrails, from which the liver was deftly cut free to be put on a plate for divination.

Divining a pig's liver can be as complex as astrology, but its elements are simple. The left hemisphere pertains to the gods, and the right to man. Ideally the flesh is healthy and firm, and the bile duct well-inflated. This indicates a prosperous future for the individual whose fate is being divined. To improve their chances, the Iban only sacrifice young and apparently healthy pigs. The only badly diseased liver I saw was on the Batang Ai when a pig was killed for a distinguished head-hunter called Mani. It was blotched and shrunken, and Mani, as it happened, was terminally ill. The subtleties of divination lie between these two extremes, in deciding the meaning of minor blemishes and indentations of the flesh. A brief glance at the steaming organ suggested that Jingga and his family could look forward to the future with some confidence, but my hangover did not permit detailed examination.

A few yards away the bards circled round the pillars of the gallery and chanted of the search for Singalang Burong:

'Have you seen the seed of the shrine decorated with tassels
of human hair?
Have you seen the seed which is red like a blooming flower?'

Some hours later the hornbill took flight. It was slotted into the top of the pole which had been prepared for it, a solid tree trunk, which was then carefully manoeuvred off the end of the platform and into a hole dug for it so that it stood like a flagpole beside the longhouse. Decorated with flowers and flags, the hornbill was assumed to go flying to the ends of the earth to find Jingga's wealth, and as though a load of responsibility had been removed, the festival then turned to comedy.

In a mirror image of the day before, more warriors appeared at the top of the ladder, but this time they were girls dressed quite grotesquely as men. In suits and shirts they strutted across the gallery where *tuak* was pressed upon them by simpering maidens with bass voices who had trouble keeping their sarongs knotted round their muscular chests. They paraded up the gallery, preceded by a matronly bard and followed by a shambling caricature of Jingga, hugely padded at the belly and dragging instead of his pig an empty bottle of arak.

Undisturbed by this display and the giggling crowd which followed, the bards sang of Singalang Burong's response to the invitations:

'I will not attend a feast in the land where red clouds form
Until I have seen brains spattered all over the jar.'

As the day wore on the pigs' corpses on the platform swelled up to oval balloons in the heat, and their bloody mouths stretched to black, mocking grins. A boy, heavily made up with lipstick and eyeshadow, offered *tuak* to a girl who wore trousers and sported a charcoal moustache. A fighting cock tiptoed up to a sleeping dog and pecked it viciously on the tail so that it ran howling down the gallery.

Down on the beach where a fire glowed brightly in the gathering dusk, the nasal drone could still be heard from the longhouse:

'Then the slack old skin of the drums is replaced with that of
a Kayan,
Tautened with toggles made from the bones of his fingers.'

The lamps were lit inside the gallery and illuminated another feast of meat and another flood of *tuak*, but this time it was the women who offered up the prayers for increase. The next morning the bloodstains on the platform had turned dark brown, and dogs slept amidst a litter of rice and palm leaves. A small boy urinated on a dog, the dog urinated on a mat, and no one paid attention. A great weariness reigned. The gallery was strewn with sleeping bodies. Gobs of red betel and fragments of food littered the floor. Empty bottles of arak were rolled against the pillars, and buckets of *tuak* stood unattended by apartment doors. Through the debris the bards still wandered, and now the seeds in Singalang Burong's skulls were behaving like lovers:

'The last of the seeds to be planted are sitting, passing a lighted
cigarette from hand to hand,
The first of the seeds to be planted are lounging with infants
in their laps.'

In desultory fashion people began to rouse themselves. Ading started to mend a torn net. Two girls amused a child by banging on a gong. Mandau's wife swept up her section of the gallery. The offerings were taken down from their poles and from the loft. Still the bards paraded, but now the seed was flourishing and multiplying;

'The seed is seen to be people, sitting and talking widely
together,
The seed is seen to be people, standing and reminiscing in
ringing voices.'

It was time for Singalang Burong and his company to return to heaven.

7

Keeping Cool

AT SOME POINT during the *gawai kenyalang* Danggang reappeared
in the longhouse. I missed the noise of the outboard, but about
a day before the festival ended, a discordant syncopation entered
the monotonous one-two-three beat of the bards' chanting. The
two-man chorus, which was supposed to listen to each line
chanted by the leader and echo the words and rhythm, suddenly
took on a nasal tone and their staves jingled with a livelier beat,
one-*two*, one-*two*, one-*two*.

A lumpy expression came into the face of the senior, $15 bard
as he heard his words and his beat being upset and elaborated
on by two newcomers. Throughout the festival, relays of per-
formers had occupied the chorus's undemanding and repetitive
role, but this pair was different and among the exhausted guests
there was a ripple of interest. It was as though a dull pianist had
been upstaged by a scintillating percussion and bass. The upstarts
were Danggang and Limbang, and from their mischievous looks,
it was apparent that they were out to show the backwoodsmen
of the Bangkit how a sacred chant should be delivered.

In this they undoubtedly succeeded. The old man became
increasingly disconcerted and the crowd gathered round to listen
to the competition. It continued until Danggang saw an opportunity to take over the lead from another bard further up the
gallery. A little group followed him – proof of his superiority –
but Ngali was not impressed. Art might impel Danggang to

111

excellence, but *adat* or custom law required him to conform.

'If a man goes to a faraway place,' he said later, 'he should follow the *adat* of that place and not his own.'

This was sound advice, and I could wish that he had said it at the time. In the dry-mouthed aftermath of brandy and arak, washed down by buckets of *tuak*, I had begun to wonder whether Jingga's *gawai* was the one to present as a model to the outside world. There had been Michael's collapse, the iridescent rugs, Bulik's shambolic performance, and the self-conscious giggles of the young warriors. All that was worrying, and now I realised from Danggang's behaviour that there were shortcomings in the bard as well. My doubts turned to gloom, but as usual it was difficult to find the right criteria to judge what Time-Life wanted.

Jingga's festival might not have been first-rate, but it was absolutely authentic, and it could be argued that a second-rate one was a great deal more representative of festivals in general. On the other hand it would hardly satisfy Lou's demands for beauty. And suppose we turned a blind eye to the rugs and the pedestrian chanting, would that not land us in the T-shirt trap once more? My gloom came close to despair. We were due to attend a longhouse meeting to discuss our request for staying on after the festival and now I was beginning to doubt whether we were right to have chosen this community in the first place.

We had suggested to Langga the headman that we should pay $1,000 Malay a week for the right to stay. Although it sounded generous, the money had to cover the sort of inconvenience that might be expected from the intrusion of a photographer and a journalist, not to mention the emotional disturbance caused by the presence of three extremely bad-tempered Europeans. Wearily I recognised that the last item made it cheap at the price, and that any move was impossible. There was little chance of us agreeing on anything, but none at all of agreeing to look for another longhouse.

Ngali had said nothing about Danggang's behaviour, because he was ill. He waited until the end of the festival then told Michael that he was suffering from diarrhoea which had been made worse by a pill which one of the Europeans had given him. As it happened his timing could scarcely have been worse. All that bound the Europeans together at that moment was annealing hostility. Michael was still recovering from his fever, and with the delicate precision of an invalid had managed to tweak our nerve-ends so that we could hardly speak for fury.

In the afternoon Tony had set himself to photograph the praus drawn up on the beach until Michael came to sit beside them, his pink nose and flashing spectacles handicapping any attempt to portray them as artefacts untouched by the encroachment of the modern world. That evening he nudged me out of a deep sleep with his foot, saying as I opened my eyes, 'I just thought I'd tell you that it was a really interesting longhouse meeting you decided to miss.' I gazed up at the unshaven red bristle round his chin and thought of murder.

A little later Ngali came to complain about the pill, and Michael reached our level of anger effortlessly. With eyes flashing, he accused me of administering the wrong drug to Ngali, and when I furiously denied even having spoken to the old hero let alone having diagnosed his complaint and prescribed a remedy, he returned to Ngali and explained that Tony and I were fools. Even though he spoke in Iban, the import of his words was unmistakable.

'Are you saying we're fools?' I snarled. 'You've no right to say that.'

'Of course you're a fool.' he snapped. 'The Iban were your responsibility while I was ill, and look what happens. You're both fools.'

This argument could have run and run, but I saw Langga coming down the gallery towards us and bottled up my rage.

'You're sick,' I said icily. 'You don't know what you're saying and I refuse to give any weight to your words.'

It was a good exit line, and I turned away. I had scarcely gone ten yards before Michael called me back. I returned sulkily.

'Langga wants us to attend the longhouse meeting now,' he said in a brittle voice.

The heads of families were waiting for us in Langga's apartment. As we entered, Michael was shaking from the effects of his fever, I was shaking with rage, and Tony was preserving the studied aloofness which he had practised since his return from Kuching.

By a remarkable feat of self-control, Michael explained in a husky voice what we wanted to do and why we wanted to stay. Langga replied that he personally was happy to have us there, but some of the heads of families were concerned that we had not made our intentions known before. He asked us to wait outside while they discussed our offer. We stood in angry silence not looking at each other until we were summoned back to be told that the longhouse had decided that we might stay. Michael then asked me to say something by way of reply. In a voice constricted with fury, I dredged up such clichés as could be found in my congested mind.

'We are delighted to be allowed to stay because you have such a wonderful longhouse' – 'I've already said that,' snapped Michael, breaking off from his translation – 'and we were particularly touched by your warm welcome at the *gawai kenyalang*' – 'Tell them something they haven't heard' – 'and we look forward to getting to know you better' – 'At least try to use concepts they understand' – 'in the weeks ahead, and let me conclude by saying – for God's sake, Michael, *shut up*! – how happy we are to be here.'

I tried to guess from their dark, attentive faces how much of this murderous interchange had come through. Perhaps it simply had the peremptory tone that Iban itself had. Most of the faces looked happy enough, but Langga's expression was veiled.

In essence Langga's function as headman was to preserve the harmony of the longhouse. The lack of privacy meant that all quarrels became public and created a general sense of disturbance. To avoid such an outcome was his responsibility, not just because it produced an uncomfortable atmosphere, but because it aroused a correspondingly disturbed state in the spiritual world. The longhouse would become 'hot', and ill-luck would befall it.

Michael had in fact good reason for his abrasiveness. His illness had left him weak, yet he still had to shoulder the responsibility for settling us into the longhouse, and without James who had not yet returned from his parents' *gawai*, the burden of translation fell to him alone. But a far more insidious worry was gnawing at his vitals.

Having made him a warrior in the *gawai kenyalang*, Jingga evidently now expected him to do the right thing by Aching. And so did Aching. At mealtimes she would now rest her thigh on his, and on one significant occasion while she was cooking supper she burnt the rice, news of which flew round the longhouse almost before the charred grains had been scraped from the pot. There was general agreement among the women, although it took them hours of audible debate to produce it, that burning the food like that was a sure sign that a girl was in love. Resolutely Michael insisted that one wife was enough, but his reluctance to do the decent thing bewildered Jingga's ancient, grey-haired mother, Munoh. 'Why don't you just go to bed with her?' she demanded impatiently.

Even without Aching, the strain of reconciling reality with Time-Life's preconceptions of it would have produced a simmering tension, but with her we frothed and boiled.

She was an adopted child. This was not uncommon among the Iban: of thirty children under the age of fifteen in the longhouse, twelve were adopted, and in nearly every case the children were already closely related to their new parents. Thus Mandau had adopted his own grandson, Langga's eldest child, to provide a support for his old age, while Aching was Jingga's natural niece, the child of his sister who had left the longhouse following a divorce. Aching, however, had grown up to be a wilful girl who preferred the bright lights of Kapit to the oil lamps of the longhouse, and gossip accused her of earning a living on the streets. Now her husband had deserted her, leaving her with two children. The elder was adopted, but she took the younger, two-

115

year-old Sulang, with her when she returned to the longhouse. Yet she was clearly unhappy there, and the arrival of the Time-Life men must have seemed to offer a way out. However strange and quarrelsome they were, they had at least the merit of novelty.

After a false start, she and her family had fixed on Michael as the best bet. With anyone less scrupulous their problem might have been solved, but scruples were part of what made Michael so uncomfortable as a companion. To see the Iban packaged for mass consumption rubbed him raw, and quite apart from his considerations for his own family, the idea that he might be exploiting Aching in any way was, I suspected, no less repugnant to him. And so while Aching moped over her rejection, and I brooded over my bruised ego, Jingga plotted to break down Michael's resistance, and after each new attempt Michael emerged with his temper abraded to a new pitch of savagery.

Once the longhouse decided to accept us, our large party was divided up to spread both the burden of hospitality and the rewards. All the families within the longhouse were related to their neighbours, but the closest bonds were between the three richest families who lived in the centre. The link was provided by three beautiful sisters. Each was so stunningly good look-ing she could have appeared on the cover of *Vogue*, had she been able to spare the time from poling a dugout, planting rice or clearing jungle undergrowth from a hillside. They had besides the advantage of being the daughters of Mandau the augurer and his wife, Mangan, the wealthiest couple in the house.

In the normal course of events, the life of an augurer was the same as anyone else's in the longhouse, but before a major undertaking such as the choice of farm-sites for the following year, he became an intermediary between the community and the spiritual world. It was Mandau's responsibility to seek the right omen bird – for farming a cheerful, bobbing bird called a White-rumped Sharma which looked like a red-breasted magpie but sang with the liquid beauty of a nightingale – and on hearing it to cut a branch which preserved the power of the omen. This

'A woman will favour such a man': the tattooed hands of a successful
head-hunter

The platform at Rumah Langga at the break of day with a woman returning from the river

The bawdy women of Nanga Bretik driving fish towards a trap: Bangan at the far end

Vogue cover girl and mother of six: the exquisite Sebang about to
make the pole bend

Ngali, last of the Iban war-leaders, victorious both in the Second World War and in the War of the Penises

The first bathe of the day at the women's pool

Langga with his fighting cock: proud, acquisitive and morally
prepared to take a head

Tony protected at last from the midday sun, and consuming a Dutch Baby

(*below*) The bard: Danggang momentarily free of dark glasses and jockey cap

The dance: Min sinuously holding Iban attention and enflaming European passions

The dance continued: Michael displaying the customary reluctance
before being frog-marched on to the floor

The dance concluded: the author demonstrating the benefits of Miss
Buchanan's Highland dancing classes

'A farting drink': Jingga downs another glass of *tuak* from Mangan as he parades the *kenyalang* up the gallery

(*opposite*) The *kenyalang* comes home from the Caves of Thunder: Jingga carries the effigy along the platform

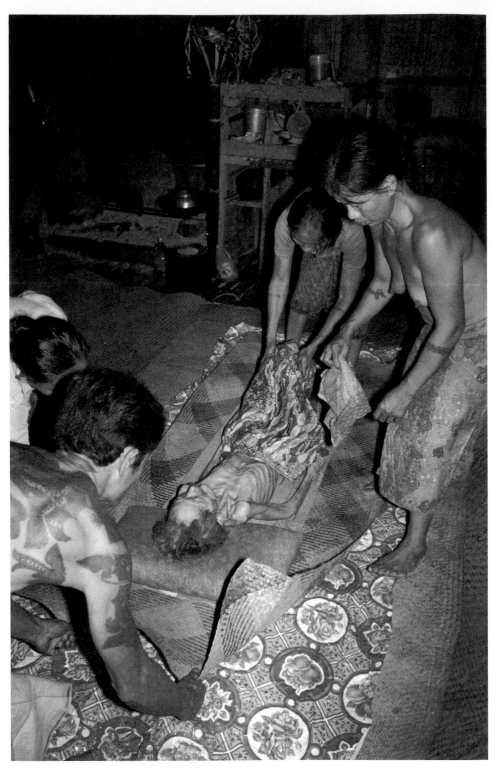

Saul coming home: the old woman's body laid out after her death, her
ghost presumably hovering nearby

omen stick was then used in all the rituals which concerned the farm during the year.

The purpose of all omens and dreams, good or bad, was benign, he insisted. They pointed to the proper course of conduct to be followed, but it remained the responsibility of the person concerned to act appropriately. This sense of responsibility was best shown in hard work, a capacity which, he let it be understood, some possessed in greater measure than others.

'In all my life I have never been short of rice,' he observed when the great outpouring of rice offerings and rice wine was over, 'but you have to work hard. Last year I spent most of my time at my farm away from the longhouse in order to keep pests away from the rice. Some families lost nearly all their crops from pigs and monkeys. I had a good harvest, but you must work hard.'

His position as augurer was a sign that he possessed all the virtues which the upriver Iban valued most highly, but to an outsider the clearest sign of his merit was his wife. Mangan was a fireball of energy. Loud-voiced, raw-boned and incapable of sitting idle for a moment, she made even her husband appear work-shy. Not only was she always the first out in the morning to fetch water for cooking, and the first to be down at the river washing clothes, she was also the first to help others with their work if they were sick or short-handed. It was typical of her to come to the help of Lagok's wife, and to make her sympathy forcefully known. Indeed, whenever there was a longhouse meeting, she would shout her opinions from the edge of the circle loud enough to be heard above any other argument, and when there was music being played, her raucous comments about her own and the other musicians' inability to beat time on a gong almost drowned the sound of the orchestra. To say that Mangan was admirable only conveyed the half of it; she was also generous, warm-hearted and utterly lovable.

If her daughters had the good sense to take after their father in looks, it was from her that the good sense came. Since they had also inherited much of her generosity of character, they

117

must have had their pick of available men when they came to be married. One had gone to live in her husband's longhouse, but the three at Rumah Langga had all done well.

The eldest, Gi, had married a hard-working man who was employed at the oilfields at Miri. Sebang, the middle daughter, was the wife of Langga, while the youngest, Orin, was married to Jingga's son Bulik. With Langga's apartment on one side, and Jingga's on the other, Mandau and Mangan were, therefore, at the centre of the longhouse both genealogically and physically, and in their behaviour they appeared to be equally satisfied with their daughters' choices.

There was, however, one significant indication that they did not regard their neighbours with equal esteem. Because only the width of a single plank separated one apartment from another, it was usual for friends and still more so for relatives to remove a section of the wall so that they could talk to each other or even climb through into each other's apartment. The size of the gap was an accurate measure of the intimacy between the two families, and a sudden quarrel would result in some quick carpentry to repair the wall. On Jingga's side the space was no bigger than the size of a small picture frame, but between Mandau and Langga there was a hole in the wall big enough for a person to step through.

Mandau's respect for Langga was well-founded. His grandfather had come to the Bangkit in 1915, and although every ten or fifteen years since then a new longhouse had been built, usually within a few miles of the old, the community had almost always chosen as its headman someone from his family. The position was not hereditary, but Langga's grandfather, uncle and brother had all held the position before him.

He was tall and good-looking, a man of deep passion and considerable shrewdness. He was easily carried away by his own stories, and at such times his normally quiet voice would grow louder and louder until its harsh, ranting tones carried the length of the gallery. Dark eyes glowing fiercely, he would lift his face so that his teeth were bared, and he seemed to be defying an army of enemies even when the tale only concerned an argument he had had with a Chinese shopkeeper. The other side of that passionate nature was revealed when Dibit, his youngest son, fell sick. For two days, Langga looked after him with fierce devotion, cradling him in the lap of his sarong, or rocking him in his arms and soothing him with a soft murmur.

In his capacity as headman, he behaved quite differently. He spoke little, and when he did his voice was quiet and deliberative. Although the longhouse was known as Rumah Langga or Langga's longhouse, he could not even consider himself first among equals. His position in the fiercely egalitarian society of the longhouse carried prestige without power. In their attempt to create some form of administrative system among the Iban, the Brookes had elevated the post to make the headman the intermediary between the government and the longhouse. The government expected him to enforce their regulations, while the longhouse expected him to settle disputes satisfactorily and to maintain a calm atmosphere in the community. All this had to be accomplished solely by his personal influence, derived in large part from his knowledge of customary law or *adat*.

When almost one hundred self-confident, assertive people live in the close confines of a longhouse, there is clearly a good chance that arguments may boil over, especially during the drunken atmosphere of a festival. That they did not was greatly to Langga's credit, nevertheless I did not find him a sympathetic personality. In the distribution of bodies, I would have preferred to be with Mandau and the wonderful Mangan. They drew Tony, however, and since Jingga held on firmly to Michael, Langga got me.

This division meant that the Time-Life trio saw less of each other, and the worst of the tension could be avoided. However, I had still to get Michael to interpret for me, which he never shirked, and Tony and I had to ensure that our activities coincided. Now that the *gawai kenyalang* was in the bag for good or ill, a succession of chapters and essays stretched in front of us about hunting, farming, fishing and weaving; someone had to be picked for 'A Day in the Life'; the women had to be cajoled into co-operation for 'The Women's Day'; and somehow the children had to be persuaded to behave naturally for 'The Children' while three large Europeans hung over them interviewing, interpreting and photographing.

For the women and children, my own preference would have been to concentrate on Langga's family, and especially his wife, the lovely Sebang. She was not quite as beautiful as her elder sister, Gi, but her warmth and directness enchanted me. It was a hopeless passion, yet while it lasted every aspect of her seemed utterly desirable, from her thick black hair and clear brown eyes to her fine-boned ankles and tiny feet. I used to invent excuses to spend time in the apartment with her. '*Aku ka ngirop*' – 'I want to drink' – I would cry in what I hoped was an appealing manner, or in moments of high emotion, '*Aku ka ngirop* Dutch Baby', which was intended to sound like an endearment although it referred also to a chocolate drink we had brought up from Song. Occasionally she could be persuaded to take a carton of Dutch Baby herself, and I would try to make headway with the few Iban sentences that Michael had drilled into me. Since they were all aimed at establishing genealogies – a task which I found tedious but which the Iban and anthropologists revelled in – I could only say with burning intensity, '*Sapah nama apai ngo brapa rega anak?*' – 'What is the name of your father and how many children do you have?' As love talk, it had limitations.

The Iban did not actually employ the Victorian term, poodle-faker, but it expressed precisely what they thought of a man who spent too much time with women in the apartment instead of being out on the gallery or working in the open air. The interesting longhouse meeting I had missed through being asleep had been held to fine Alo, a seventeen-year-old boy, for flirting with a married woman. No doubt he was more successful than I, for all I achieved was the slightly unbelievable information that this sylph-like woman had given birth to no fewer than six children, the last of whom was an eighteen-month-old girl called Suda.

Everyone loved Suda. Plump, smiling and docile, she seemed to epitomise what an Iban child should be. She was the favourite of the other children, the women doted on her, and in the evening when the men sat out on the gallery to gossip, she would lie cradled in her father's saronged lap, contentedly clutching his finger. When she walked on the slatted floor of the longhouse, an art most children did not master until they were two, her tottering steps held everyone entranced, especially Limau.

Limau was a round and jolly woman with a coarse tongue, grey hair, gold teeth and lips which were perpetually betel-red. Living next door to Langga, she used to look after Suda while the couple were farming, and she had appointed herself the child's chief worshipper. If Suda tramped stolidly over to watch someone mend a net, Limau would be crawling just behind gurgling, 'Are you walking? Who's walking?' If Suda squatted over an opening in the floor (and the inconvenience of the slats in walking was compensated for by their convenience in toilet-training), Limau would be on her knees cooing, 'Are you peeing? Is that you peeing?' No one seemed to find this excessive, quite the contrary. During a ritual she stumbled into a row of plates containing a rice offering, with Limau at her heels cackling, 'Are you making an offering too?' and both spectators and celebrant joined in with cries of 'Look, Suda's making an offering.'

Although Suda was a particular favourite, it was generally true that children could do no wrong. Whatever trouble they got into, they were rarely scolded. A fight was stopped by the simple expedient of removing the smaller child from the conflict. If they were unduly noisy or tugged their parents' hair – a favourite occupation since the hair of an adult sitting on the floor was at just the right height for a small child to pull – they were simply lifted away, and told that it was wrong. Most adults would immediately abandon whatever task they were engaged on to console an upset child, and a woman would often give her breast to a crying child to suck as a comforter.

There was a limit to this indulgence. *Adat* did not permit anyone, even children, to destroy social harmony. Tantrums were

121

forbidden. Uncontrolled screaming upset everyone, and more importantly bothered the spirits. When Pirak, an eight-year-old girl, lost control of herself one day and refused to stop crying, she was hustled out on to the platform where a basket was pushed over her head and a bucket of water emptied over her. The shock silenced her for a moment, then she began sobbing again. At once Limau drew a bush-knife from its scabbard and rushed over to her, laying the naked blade against her forehead, and then her neck. Like the water, the application of iron was presumably intended to cool her spirit, but the menace was unmistakable, and there were no more tears.

Less physical threats were also used to keep the children in order. Orin used to point at one of the Europeans, and whisper to her badly behaved four-year-old son, Nyandang, 'Be quiet, or the white spirit will come and eat you up.' On the Batang Ai, the ultimate threat was the cannibal *indai guru*, but at Rumah Langga they preferred another menace which would have given a Freudian pause for thought. When Sulang was fiercely resisting a spoonful of cough mixture we had prescribed, Jingga took the boy on his lap and said gently, 'Come on now, eat it up or we'll castrate you.' Sulang covered his eyes with his hands and took the first spoonful, but then jerked his head away again. His grandfather rubbed his cheek softly against the child's head. 'Eat it all', he murmured, 'or we'll cut your penis off.' At that moment James walked up. 'Here comes the man with the knife,' said Jingga, 'he's coming to castrate you.' Hurriedly Sulang took his medicine, like a man one might almost say, and then gazed solemn-faced at James from the crook of Jingga's encircling elbow.

Until they were about five, the children were treated much the same regardless of sex. It was true that the women loved to fondle the penises of baby boys, either nuzzling the little commas of flesh or caressing them gently between thumb and forefinger, but with that exception, boys and girls were left more or less to their own devices. From the age when they could safely negotiate the ladder, they used the river and the nearby jungle as a playground. They swam, dived from overhanging branches, fished and carved wood with razor-sharp knives. Inside the long-house they had the same games as any other children – versions of blind man's buff, chases, and playing with tops and carved toys.

From the age of seven they were supposed to go to school, but no great effort was made to persuade them to do so against their will. Langga's two boys, who were about eight and ten, refused to attend, because the nearest school was between three and five hours away, depending on the river level, and they would have had to live in a hostel during term-time. Neither Langga nor Mandau, who had adopted the elder boy, raised any objection.

The freedom which individual parents permitted their children was, however, circumscribed by the discipline exerted by the community as a whole. Even among the children themselves, comments, jokes and teasing exerted a strong pressure towards conformity, and in extreme cases their disapproval was expressed through ostracism. This in fact was what had begun to happen to Sulang.

As the excitement of the festival ebbed away, Aching took to sitting silently in one of Jingga's red plastic chairs, staring at the ceiling and resolutely ignoring Sulang who howled at her feet or tugged desperately at her arm to attract her attention. As a result he increasingly became the direct responsibility of his grandparents, and their behaviour towards him was much more typical of the way the Iban treated their children.

His grandmother, Dambak, a grey-haired, gaunt-cheeked woman, would hold him, let him scramble all over her, and when he was frightened allow him to suckle her withered breasts. To persuade him to do something he did not want to do, she resorted to guile rather than force. I once watched her spend ten fruitless minutes in cajolery and story-telling in an attempt to persuade him to wear a pair of shorts, before she finally distracted his attention sufficiently by making shadows on the wall with her fingers to let her slip them on without fuss. There were no harsh words from her however difficult he was.

123

Nevertheless, the experience of his short life had left Sulang distrustful and furious-tempered. The smallest frustration made him scowl and stamp the floor in anger. If he were not comforted, his face would slowly crumple and tears began to flow, but they were tears of rage rather than sorrow. It was Jingga who seemed best able to console him in these moods. He would gather the boy up in his huge, tattooed arms and rock him gently until the anger had spent itself. When Sulang ran into the offering pole during the festival, and began to howl in pain and anger, Jingga marched up to the pole and shook his fist threateningly at it. At once Sulang stopped crying, and looked at his grandfather as though recognising a kindred soul.

When Jingga and Dambak were occupied with tending the pepper farm or preparing the new rice fields, the other children were supposed to look after him. Usually an older girl such as Pantai, who was Sibat's adopted daughter, would be in charge of the youngsters in their parents' absence, but amongst themselves the children showed a touching concern for the cares of one another, and the sight of one of them in tears would bring the others circling round with grave faces. Only Sulang was outside this mutual assistance pact. He had cried too often for them to pay attention any more, and he would be left unattended on the floor to weep until Pantai arrived.

'What do you want?' she would ask.

Unsure of what it was he did want, he would look at her with a troubled expression.

'Do you want some fruit?'

A little uncertainly, he would nod, but almost before she had given it to him, he would realise that fruit was not what he wanted, and the tears would gather again. Exasperated, Pantai might walk him up and down for a little, but at twelve years old, she too had her responsibilities – rice to husk, hens to feed, meals to prepare, and if Sulang did not respond quickly he was left to comfort himself. Adults found him almost as great a trial as the children, and he was as a result neglected at best and shouted at or pushed away at worst.

124

At night he often woke and cried, the only time I heard that noise in the dozen longhouses I slept in. It was followed by the low murmur of Dambak's voice as she comforted him. Quite soon the sobs would come more slowly and he would go to sleep.

No member of the longhouse escaped the demands for conformity which were made by *adat*. The precepts of that body of common sense and tradition entered into every aspect of social behaviour, and if you did not accept them, you rejected the community and in the end would have to leave. Aching had already reached that stage, and the sobbing of her son showed that the same requirement was being made of him.

But the alternative was worse. Without *adat* it was impossible to live socially in the jungle, and the three Europeans were proof of that. Between us, we knew how to write, to photograph, to study foreign people, but to live with each other was beyond us. When it came to controlling our behaviour, we had no *adat* to refer to, no dreams or omens to guide us, no gods to sacrifice to. We had only the still, small voice of reason, and in the gush and surge of emotion that could hardly be heard at all.

8

The Messengers of God

LIMBANG REGARDED THE piglessness of Rumah Langga as a personal challenge. For three years no one had succeeded in killing a wild pig during the festival season. 'The dogs bark,' an old man said sadly before the *gawai kenyalang*, 'but we find nothing. We know the pigs are there. Why can't we catch them?'

The question might have been designed expressly to tempt Limbang. In the days since he had left his government-built longhouse, his face had gradually lost its sallow hue and tired look. Like someone recovered from a long illness, there seemed no limit to his renewed zest for pleasure. A river of *tuak* disappeared down his throat and still his eyes would search thirstily for the source. A golgotha of bones mounted beside his plate, but he continued to pick hungrily at the carcass.

Even before the festival ended, we had begun to eat the sacrificial pigs. The first of them was roasted by Danggang who hovered over the flames like a sorcerer until the corpse had been scorched all over, and then in a gloom relieved only by the kitchen fire seven or eight of us sat round and tore it to pieces with our bare hands. It was not one of the great meals of my life. Limbang who was squatting beside me helped me find some of the soft, sweet flesh from the cheek, but it was attached to some crackling which had the consistency of elephant hide. After chewing unavailingly at it for some minutes, I dropped it through the slats of the floor, surreptitiously as I thought except that

Limbang nudged me. 'Not good?' he asked. I patted my stomach in a pantomime of satisfaction. 'Very good.' I exclaimed, and by way of confirmation leant forward to tear some more meat from the pig's cheek. A pale marble came away with the flesh which I bit into. It was crisp on the outside and slippery on the inside. Unwilling to betray any further signs of weakness, I chewed remorselessly on until it disintegrated. Long before I finally rendered it swallowable I knew what it was, and when a flare from the fire revealed a hollow eye-socket beside the pig's snout I felt no sicker than before.

Beside me Limbang never stopped. He demolished most of a shoulder, ripped apart the meat on a foreleg, and sucked juicily on the bone. His appetite was in the truest sense gargantuan, yet it paled beside his lust for hunting.

In nearly all the upriver Iban we had met, hunting was a passion. Even the poorest families kept a pack of three or four dogs for hunting pig, as well as a shotgun for deer, or a spear for anything on four legs. Venison, wild pork and jungle fowl supplied a crucial part of their diet, but even James whose supply of food was as assured as ours found the challenge irresistible. To be deprived of it as Limbang had been was to lose the savour of life.

When the platform of the Katibas longhouse collapsed, Limbang had reached the victims some way ahead of us. 'Anyone hurt?' was his first question. 'Anyone out pig-hunting?' was his second. In the years since he had moved from the headwaters of the Delok river, he had had few opportunities for hunting. A marauding honey bear might raid the farms, and deer might devastate the fields at harvest-time, but real hunting – stalking silently through the jungle in search of a buck, or tearing headlong after a pack of barking dogs on the scent of a wild boar – there had been little of that.

Two days after the longhouse had agreed to let us stay, Limbang at last had the opportunity to gratify his deepest desire. He chose as his partner Nyanggau, who lived in one of the poorer apartments near the downriver end of the longhouse. He was a

slow, even-tempered man, and a distant relative. More importantly he kept a pack of five dogs.

They were typical of the breed: about fourteen inches high at
the shoulder, tan-coloured, and smooth-haired where mange
had not left them bald. Except for Limau's husband, Inggol, who
slept with his head on his dogs, the Iban regarded them as
nuisances rather than pets. A hissing chorus of 'Tsai, tsai!' drove
off any that tried to get on a mat, and when Sulang refused to
be distracted by any other pastime, Dambak would give him a
stick, and whisper gently, 'Why don't you go and hit the dogs?'
A diet of cold rice, kicks and blows produced in them a mood of
restless lethargy. They twitched as they slept, stretched out on
window-sills or curled up under mats. Awake they scratched
and coupled until the floor bounced, and they fought at any
provocation, with bared teeth and menacing growls from the
stronger and piercing screams from the losers. It needed a hunt
to give purpose to their lives. Then they became as eager as
puppies, fearless of the danger in a wild boar's tusks which could
eviscerate them without difficulty. Several carried long grey scars
from previous encounters, and one dog in a downriver longhouse
had a ragged wound eighteen inches long and five inches wide.

Armed only with spears, Limbang and Nyanggau set off at
first light. They had borrowed four more dogs from Sibat, and
the tiny dugout which they poled upstream towards virgin jungle
seemed alive with panting tongues and wagging tails. They left
the boat in a creek, and for three or four hours travelled across
country. They moved carefully, studying the ground for tracks,
high-stepping across streams like dancers – toe-first into the
water and heel-first out of it – and listening intently for sounds
in the still air. In mid-morning a volley of barks signalled that a
dog had caught the scent of a pig, and the need for care disappeared. Immediately men and animals tore through the forest in
the direction of the sound.

Primary jungle, unlike secondary, has the merit of being rela-
tively clear of undergrowth, but barbed creepers hang down from
branches and curl out from decaying roots. The ground is rough,

and on the precipitous slopes the carpet of dead leaves is as treacherous underfoot as a bar of soap. None of this matters in pursuit of a pig. The only rule is to run flat out towards the frenzied barking. In previous years the sound had led hunters to nothing. This time it was different. The dogs had cornered a young sow against a bank. While Nyanggau fumbled with his weapon, Limbang pushed past and speared it. Its dying squeals signalled the end of the long dearth.

Delighted though he was by his success, Limbang was not entirely satisfied when he returned that evening. While the two men were eviscerating the pig, they heard the whistling call of a kingfisher. This was one of the seven birds which were identified as the sons-in-law of Singalang Burong, and for hunters its message was worth hearing for it promised that they would get game. Almost immediately it was followed by the slow, descending 'pau-pau-pau' call of another of the god's messengers, a scarlet-breasted bird with a brown back, about the size of a lapwing, which was called a Diard's Trogon. They were now in a quandary for this call meant that they should return. Taken together the two auguries needed careful interpretation.

Limbang was certain that they meant that the hunters would get more pig by retracing their tracks. In his slow and careful way, Nyanggau argued that the kingfisher's call urged the hearer to go forward in search of game, and since it came first they should follow that to begin with, and only return later. They were hunting with his dogs, and so his argument won the day. Five hours of further hunting produced nothing, however, and at last they started back towards the boat. When they came near the river, they found, to Limbang's frustration, the tracks of three more pigs. His interpretation of the omens had been correct, and had they turned back as he had argued the hunt would have been still more successful.

At the time there was no shortage of food, but later in the year, after the fruit season was over, and when heavy rains made fishing difficult, a failed or half-successful hunting trip would be more serious. Without game they might not starve, but they would be undernourished. The correct interpretation of omens was, therefore, important, and Limbang gained credit as much for reading the signs aright as for actually bringing home the meat. Nor did it escape anyone that Nyanggau was both poor and a bad interpreter of auguries.

The relationship of the hunter and the omen birds bothered me intensely. The birds were certainly the sons-in-law of Singalang Burong, but because even their most straightforward message was open to a variety of interpretations, a hunter could pick the one which best fitted with his own judgement of the situation. Success proved the veracity of a favourable omen, but failure did not disprove it. Either the hunter's understanding was faulty, or the omen was referring to some other event. Thus when James and Ading went after pig back on the Batang Ai, they too heard the auspicious call of a kingfisher but caught nothing. James, however, narrowly missed stepping on a venomous snake, and Ading immediately commented that the bird must have been referring to his escape rather than to their finding game.

The advantage of such an approach was that it explained any contradiction between subjective perceptions and objective truths. A man might be certain that he had aimed his gun straight, but the deer could gallop off unharmed. A woman might believe that she had boiled the rice properly and still find that it had burned. The fault lay in the bad omen, whether bird or dream, and a person's confidence in his or her ability remained unimpaired. Langga provided a shameless example a few weeks later when he went hunting and missed an easy shot at two pigs. What a Western observer might have taken to be poor marksmanship was, he immediately declared, the result of a jay, one of the omen birds, which he had earlier heard on his left indicating poor hunting.

I gradually came to the conclusion that in the Iban cosmology the supernatural world took the place that the Western mind gave to unconscious wishes. The energy and time that we spent on self-examination and self-doubt, the Iban directed towards the demands of spirits and gods. If that were the case, an omen bird was the revelation of an unconscious desire flying high. Obviously it was easy to cheat, but the fact was that people like Ngali and Mandau who observed the omens closely did better than those who did not, like Jingga and Nyanggau.

It was not an entirely satisfactory explanation, and in some ways it seemed more appropriate to explain *our* situation in *Iban* terms. Ever since the festival began, I had started to sense that Time-Life was our Singalang Burong, and Lou the most notable of his sons-in-law. Because we had no expertise in interpreting his calls, the chances of a misfortune on the scale of Jingga's harvest rose to dangerous levels. It was true that we had finally landed up in a longhouse which looked right, but that only brought into higher relief the other decisions we should soon have to make: on a hunting trip, how many spears would be needed before we could show a rifle? Out fishing, how many nets to a harpoon-gun? In the forest, how many axes and adzes to a chainsaw? In short, the old question would not go away, how many parts of resistance to one of encroachment constituted a Wild People?

Fortunately, Inyang the weaver decided to set up her loom once the departure of guests began to leave enough space. There could never have been a simpler device, indeed I found a drawing of just such a loom in the *Encyclopaedia Britannica* used to illustrate the earliest form of weaving several millennia ago. It consisted of two poles twelve feet long and separated by two thirty-inch crosspoles. To maintain the tension of the warp, or longitudinal threads, Inyang simply leant back against a sling attached to the nearer cross-piece, while the further one was tied to the longhouse wall. She was making a *puah* or blanket, which incorporated a variety of stick-like white figures on a reddish background, and to weave each crossways thread, over and under the warp, took forty-five minutes.

The splay of white threads and Inyang's intent face made it beautiful to look at, and laying aside his apparent resentment of Michael's advice, Tony photographed it in detail. It meant less to me than it should have, for somewhere in that slow interweaving, the spirits of fertility were being tied into place. That it could work was certain. Inyang had once woven a blanket incorporating fidelity for a wife with a wandering husband, which only had to be flapped in his face to put him in mind of monogamy. But of foetid heavings, strangled moans, and dark Lawrentian pulsations, I could sense nothing, only the snail-like progression of the shuttle over and under the warp, over and under, over and under.

It was the hunt that I looked forward to most. When Limbang explained how he had shouldered past Nyanggau, I immediately thought of the boar-hunt in T. H. White's *The Sword in the Stone*, when Wart and Kay and Master Twytti, the royal huntsman, went out with spears after wild boar, and I wanted to do the same.

There was no lack of hunters, for Limbang's success had transformed Rumah Langga. After his hunt, men went out with dogs and spears almost every day and came back with game. The spoils were divided according to a well-established formula which ensured that everyone shared in the good fortune; the head of the animal went to the owner of the most dogs; the liver and haunches belonged to the hunters, and the remainder was divided among the other dog-owners and the rest of the long-house.

The flesh of a wild pig was infinitely preferred to that of domesticated animals. The texture was not greasy but firm and slightly dry with a gamey flavour. So long as I avoided dining with the majority dog-owner who would serve up the head, I found it enjoyable, but more to my taste was the venison which began to appear as well. The day after Limbang's hunt, Engkin, a young man from the upriver end of the longhouse, stalked and shot a sambhur deer, whose flesh was as tender as though its most strenuous exercise had been to browse on young shoots. On the whole this was a minority taste, but there was enough meat of every kind for people to experiment.

Despite their generosity in inviting us to eat with them, the hunters seemed curiously reluctant to let us hunt with them.

They did not have enough room in the prau, they would be leaving too early, they might not leave at all. Although they did not say so, it was too intense a pleasure to share with strangers.

By way of compensation, I tried to persuade Langga to take me farming with him. On this point our auguries had been unequivocal. 'As we understand it, rice or *padi* as they call it, is absolutely crucial to Iban life,' Gillian had said. 'It's really more important than head-hunting. So we want a good, strong chapter on every aspect of its cultivation, from sowing to harvesting. Make it lively, plenty of anecdotes and lots of information. Of course, you're going at the wrong time of year and they won't actually be doing anything very interesting while you're there.' And she laughed merrily. 'But try not to make that too obvious.'

Langga betrayed no enthusiasm for my company in the jungle. In fact I had the clear impression that from his point of view even our presence in the longhouse was something to be endured. The swirl of emotion caused by our arguments and Jingga's hopes of an anthropological son-in-law did no good for the tranquillity of the longhouse, and it was a sign that things were out of joint when the guests were delayed from leaving the festival by an inauspicious omen, in this case the call of a barking deer. It was clear that he did not relish the thought of having us around during the crucial rites which marked out his farm.

His reluctance was understandable. According to Professor Derek Freeman, the ultimate authority on Iban agriculture, it was not simply a crop that he intended to grow, but a being whose qualities were remarkably like himself. In search of evidence of unitary thinking among the Iban, I had in fact marked a passage which Freeman quoted from Sir James Frazer's *The Golden Bough*:

'They explain the phenomena of reproduction, growth, decay and death in the rice on the same principles on which they explain the corresponding phenomena in human beings. They imagine that in the fibres of the plant, as in the body of a man, there is a certain vital element, which is so far independent of the plant that it may for a time be completely separated from it

133

without fatal effects, though if its absence be prolonged beyond certain limits the plant will wither and die. This vital yet separable element is what, for the want of a better word, we must call the soul of the plant . . .'

In the songs which the bards had sung during the *gawai kenyalang*, the seed had been born allegorically out of a human skull; once planted it would undergo in less than twelve months an entire life-cycle, growing, reproducing and dying, and ending once more in a human skull when it was eaten.

According to Freeman, the Iban treated the *padi* seed as though it were doing this on their behalf, living and giving itself up to death so that they should survive and prosper. Other gods might be summoned with yells and their offerings presented as though they were bribes, but the rice spirit received an affection and reverence which was rarely equalled elsewhere. When it was being planted, the last seed left in the basket was comforted so that it should not become lonely and unhappy; at harvest-time the smaller ears of rice were cossetted and cut with particular care, a process made easier by their habit of cutting each ear individually; and once they had been harvested the individual grains were heaped together because it was assumed they liked company. Rice was a reflection of the Iban themselves, and when an Iban died, it was believed in some communities that the soul after living for a short time away from the body was eventually transformed into dew which nourished the growing rice. And so the cycle was complete.

I should see none of this, so my good, strong chapter was going to have to be skewed heavily towards the opening moves in a lengthy game. Usually it began in early June when a section of forest was marked out and the trees felled. About six weeks later the dead wood was burnt, and catch crops of cucumber, maize and tobacco were sown among the embers. Then different strains of rice allowing for early and late harvesting were planted, and the last to go into the ground was the sacred rice which each family adopted as its own particular strain, containing a spirit special to them. The next five months were occupied with weeding and pest patrolling until in late February the harvest began and often continued into April.

To my relief, Mandau agreed readily enough to take me farming with him. Perhaps, as the augurer he felt more confident in his relationship with the spirits, but unlike Langga who was going to clear virgin forest with unpredictable spirits, he was also proposing to return to land which he had worked before and now considered to be ready for farming again.

'I had a good harvest there last time,' Mandau said. 'That was twelve years ago. The longhouse does quite well for land – there is a lot of primary forest, and as a result we don't have to go back to the old farms too soon.'

Since it took twelve years for the secondary jungle which sprang up to become mature and regenerate the soil, this pause was ecologically essential, but so long as the forest was allowed to renew itself, the cycle of cultivation could be repeated endlessly. Mandau was therefore following an efficient and productive means of using Sarawak's otherwise inhospitable landscape; and because he cleared only about four acres a year, the total amount of land he needed was no more than that of a smallholder in Europe. It would make an excellent chapter, and I only hoped that Mandau would clear his land in as backward and unmodernised a manner as possible.

Shortly before our arrival at Rumah Langga, the two main sites for farming had been decided on at a longhouse meeting. Both were upriver, but while one was a day's journey from the Bangkit, the other lay up a small stream and could be reached by boat in an hour. Most families had chosen the first site because they had farmed in the area the previous year and had built a temporary farmhouse there to avoid the long journey back and forth. Langga, Mandau and Jingga had chosen to farm on either side of the small stream.

In common with the majority of Iban, Mandau did not hide his opinion that Europeans were physically so incompetent as to be dangerous. Though two-year-old children were allowed to romp up and down the gallery carrying naked bush-knives

135

almost as long as themselves, their parents winced visibly if we so much as drew one from its scabbard. When I stepped into his prau the next morning with his daughter, Gi, and her husband, Mandau's first action was to tell me to sit down. The stream on which his farm stood had a particularly vicious rapid but when I ventured to stand up with a pole in my hand to give some help, his muscular son-in-law, Bindin, lent forward and thrust me into the bottom of the prau.

There was nothing to indicate why Mandau should have chosen this particular bit of forest rather than any other. From the little beach where we tied up, the land rose to form a steep bowl packed with trees growing up to seventy feet tall. The floor, amounting to one-tenth of the area, could be described as merely sloping, but the rest was steep hillside which in places became an escarpment. Over this inhospitable ground, Mandau, his son-in-law, Bindin, and Gi, the most beautiful of all his stunning daughters, performed a remarkable axe dance.

Mandau worked his way along the contour lines while Bindin moved up and down the hill. Each would select a group of trees growing so close that their branches were knitted together by a tangle of creepers and branches. With a flurry of blows, they half-cut through the trunks of all but the tree highest up the slope. Finally that too was attacked. Standing in the cool shade, I watched a small patch of blue sky open up in the green canopy overhead as the highest tree began to topple. Slowly the crown tilted until it fell against its neighbour below. That tottered and creaked until the half-severed trunk snapped and they both cannoned into the others. With a tremendous tearing of creepers and cracking of branches, the whole group heeled over one after the other in a gigantic version of the domino theory and crashed to the ground far beneath. Where six tall trees had stood, there was now only a green snowstorm of leaves and bright sunlight pouring into the clearing. But before the last leaf reached the ground, Mandau was cutting into the next tree along the line of the bowl. Meanwhile Bindin had set off his own row of dominoes further up the slope.

For much of the time, Mandau's lean body and grey hair only came into sight when Bindin's bulging torso had disappeared into another part of the forest, but when they converged the danger was immense for neither seemed willing to back off. Bindin once chopped down a seventy footer while his old father-in-law was working almost directly below. The slope was nearly one in three, and the falling tree took off as it passed the horizontal and flew through the air for several yards before hitting the ground with a thump which shook the hillside. Even though some of the twigs actually hit him, Mandau did not stop hewing. Another of Bindin's trees fell towards him, which sent him scrambling for cover, but the branches caught in those of a dead tree which split into two in mid-air and the pieces cartwheeled past on either side of him.

Bindin worked on an oil-base for much of the year, and I decided that I could wield an axe a lot less dangerously than he. Besides I felt humiliated by the episode in the prau, and by Gi's competence. All morning she strode up and down the hillside slashing away the undergrowth with a bush-knife. Her legs were smooth and white, her ankles narrow and fragile, her cheek-bones high, her brow cool, and when she strapped her bush-knife round her waist and squatted down to prepare lunch, I felt that I could no longer remain a spectator. I needed to be a participant.

When I told Mandau that I wanted to use one of his axes, his prim and serious face took on an expression I had never seen before. He laughed. It did not last long, and was partly an exclamation of disbelief, but for all that it was undoubtedly a laugh. Then he became serious once more, and tried to convince me that the power in the blade was too dangerous for me to use. I refused to be dissuaded. With a look of pure anxiety, he handed over the axe. At once Gi and Bindin ceased work and turned to watch me. I promised myself that I should try nothing too ambitious. Not a seventy footer, nor a whole clump. Just a tall, straight, solitary tree. I selected one and began to hew at it. The blade bit deep and the chips flew. It was soft wood, and the notch quickly advanced past the halfway mark. Any moment now the tree would topple, I thought, and they would see that I was a woodsman to be respected. I might follow it with a domino effect. And after that I would insist on poling the prau on the way back. With enormous vigour I continued to chop, but the tree refused to creak and lean. At last there was just a vestigial strip of bark holding the trunk together, and I finally took the elementary precaution of looking up. Fifty feet above me the branches were inextricably locked in those of a neighbouring tree. I could hack all the way through. I could swing on the trunk like a monkey – it would never fall. I turned to share the joke with the others, and Mandau took the opportunity to step forward and remove the axe from my grasp.

When we got back to the longhouse, after a humiliating journey crouched in the bottom of the prau, the story was told to a double wall of listeners. There was a lot of noise but very little dissension. Everyone agreed that the axe's spirit was not going to work for me, and that had Mandau not relieved me of it, I would surely have ended up like Simpang-Impang, a legendary figure of Iban mythology who was split up the middle and walked about in two halves.

I needed an axe of my own. Whatever happened, I would fell a tree, quickly, competently and by myself. This need coincided with several others. Tony needed to find out what Singalang Burong thought of the first batch of photographs he had sent back. Ngali needed to return to the Batang Ai to start clearing his farm. And Limbang, invigorated by a smell of the upriver life, needed to discover whether any of the members of the settlement at the Skrang scheme would join him in establishing a new longhouse far upriver and deep in primary forest.

All these added up to the overwhelming necessity of going to Sibu where axes could be bought, London telephoned, and buses caught back to the Batang Ai. Since Tony had had one visit to the fleshpots of Kuching, this was to be mine. As though it heralded a change in our fortunes, the day before my departure provided the first relaxation in our relations since our arrival on the Bangkit. Had it not been for Aching, all would have been well.

Since the end of the festival, the longhouse had begun to feel almost empty. The huge company of *praus* drawn up on the beach had disappeared, and at night the gallery no longer looked like an army barracks with bodies crammed row on row. The *tuak* had not been exhausted, and on the third day after the *kenyalang* had flown, the longhouse began drinking up what remained. Most of that belonged to the three central apartments, and the drinking began at breakfast.

The brews seemed to have taken on something of their makers' personality. Jingga's had lost its sourness, but its quality was by no means reliable; Langga's was powerful and demanding; and Mandau's, which was really made by his wife, Mangan, had a generous warmth. Small groups wandered from apartment to apartment downing it in bowls and tumblers, then returning to the gallery to gossip and doze. With the sunlight throwing bright squares through the windows, Ading hung his net from the beams so that he could begin the laborious task of tying weights to it. Inyang set up her loom, and began to knot the threads of the warp. Michael gossiped idly of anthropological scandals, and I talked about my desert island and the attraction of solitude. A great alcoholic benignity pervaded.

In the afternoon, Jingga strolled up the gallery wielding a bamboo pole like a bard's stave and spouting nonsense verse to a crowd of children who followed him as though he were the Pied Piper. Soon afterwards his wife Dambak came to fetch us to a renewed assault on the last of the *tuak* in his apartment. In the course of the festival, she had become a familiar figure. Her bony face with its deepset eyes was unexpectedly full of life, whether brooding over her four-year-old grandson, Nyandang, or guffawing open-mouthed at a joke so that two gold-capped molars at the back of her mouth gleamed in the light. Both she and Munoh, Jingga's ancient mother, had taken their turn at caring for Sulang, but the latter lacked the patience of Dambak.

Munoh was in her customary place when we entered, behind

the door where she could sit safely out of the way. Her energy remained admirable. That morning she had as usual staggered out of the apartment carying a bucket of leftover rice. With her grey hair falling round her face and her sarong in imminent danger of slipping from her waist, she had squatted on the gallery floor, and in a cracked soprano shrieked at the hens to be fed. Later she had supervised the play of her great-grandchildren, but this was done with a crumpled look on her witch's face as though unwilling to accept that she had been reduced to such a chore. When Nyandang attempted to scuttle under her arm for a reassuring pull at her withered breast, she pushed him roughly away. Her toothless, puckered mouth bulged around a wad of betel, and when she saw Michael a mischievous grin gave her sallow features the animation of a young woman.

There were about a dozen drinkers in the room, supervised by Bulik and his spoiled slender wife, Orin, For the festival, Orin had painted her short finger-nails red, but the incessant labour of cooking and washing had chipped the varnish, and now with her head bent in squinting concentration, she was rescaling the pink patches. Bulik had a bucket of *tuak* beside him, and in his amiable fashion he smiled over a cigarette and pushed a glass towards me. Despite his performance at the festival, I liked Bulik who had taken over his father's role of teaching me to speak Iban. He usually wore a pair of cotton trousers with the waistband concealed by his overhanging waist, and except for an enthusiasm for fishing seemed a stranger to any emotion stronger than geniality.

'*Ngirop, ngirop* – drink up,' he said warmly and filled the glass to the brim. During the festival, it had been difficult to drink companionably without drinking competitively, and so I grandly waved his offering away and called instead for a large bowl. It was not much of a joke, although it made Munoh cackle. It also had the effect of bringing Aching into the picture. While everyone else was seated on the floor, she had been sitting in one of the red plastic armchairs, apparently absorbed in contemplation of the ceiling. Now she rose wearily to bring a bowl from the

140

kitchen. There were shadows beneath her large eyes, and the corners of her mouth were stretched downwards. She handed the bowl to Bulik, then threw herself back into the armchair, ostentatiously ignoring Michael.

For his part, he began to engage in some basic anthropological research, by establishing the genealogy and relationships of Jingga's family. It was the start of a long series of confabulations with members of the longhouse which continued throughout our stay and eventually uncovered the family trees of all twelve families back for three or four generations. Football fans compiling a list of all-time great players betray the sort of passion that the Iban had for tracing family relationships. Thus the crucial position of Orin and her sisters linking the three central apartments emerged from a welter of information, which prompted her to raise her lovely, slightly petulant face from her nails and offer a perfect smile in acknowledgement. From her the spotlight passed to Jingga's other children, and now we learned for the first time that Aching had been adopted, after her mother left.

'Ah, poor Aching!' I exclaimed when Michael relayed the information.

This triggered a wave of comment which now aroused Aching from her study of the ceiling. Michael said something to her which made her smile sadly at me, then to my surprise and pleasure she came to sit beside me on the floor, her thigh overlapping mine. Michael laughed.

'She wants to go to bed with you,' he said.

I would gladly have believed it, but even in my inebriated state it was evident that her beseeching glances were directed at Michael. When he did not react, she jumped angrily to her feet and hurled herself back in her chair.

I thought it was something I had done, or failed to do, and felt rather as Nyanggau must have when he found that he had misinterpreted the omen bird – now what went wrong that time? From the buzz of talk, a variety of suggestions were being canvassed. The experience of listening to conversations which I

141

did not understand had taught me that the interest of the subject under discussion could be accurately determined by the number of spectators leaning through the windows from neighbouring apartments. Unless there were at least three eavesdroppers, it was rarely worth asking for a translation. On this occasion, the picture frame on Langga's side had incredibly sprouted six heads, while the vertical space one plank wide in the opposite wall was entirely filled by a column of faces. It seemed best to remain ignorant of what was being said, so I buried my nose in a bowl of Jingga's unreliable *tuak*, and tried not to imagine the sort of scathing remarks which were being directed at my clumsiness. It was a relief when the genealogies at last resumed their flow.

It was much later that Michael confessed that to deflect Aching's attentions from himself he had told her that I was infatuated with her. By then it was too late to be annoyed. In any case, Aching's problem ran far deeper than that. The traditional life upriver which delighted us and which Time-Life deemed worth paying a small fortune to have recorded, she found intolerable. The mundane tasks of pounding rice and feeding chickens bored her to distraction, and when a middle-aged farmer from a long-house downriver tried to woo her during the festival, she brushed him off rudely. That was what she had been trying to escape from when she took a shopkeeper for her first husband. Her family found her refusal to help with the chores exasperating, and the rest of the longhouse revenged themselves on her contempt for their way of life by calling her a whore. Michael thought they were right, but remembering her first beautiful praise-song to Ngali, I inclined to the romantic notion that she was an artist. The terms were not incompatible, of course, but in either event her temperament was better suited to the individual assertiveness of town life than to communal discipline upriver.

The next day she joined a boatload of departing guests to return to the bright lights of Kapit, but long before dawn the Iban and I had set off on the long journey from the Bangkit to the Premier Hotel in Sibu. It took an entire day, but the distance was immeasurable. In the course of it, Ngali the war leader,

142

Limbang the hunter, Inyang the weaver, and Danggang the bard gradually diminished in stature, and I so ineffectual in the forest was transformed into the leader, the one with the knowledge to make taxis amenable and hotels hospitable.

Compared to theirs it seemed a rather shabby, easily acquired knowledge, which separated me from them. It was shared by the rabbit-toothed Chinese girl at the reception desk who tapped confidently at a computer keyboard, and when she giggled at Danggang because he could not sign his name in the register, it became hateful.

To remember a lore so extensive that it contained all that was known about the world, and to be so immersed in myth that its phrases and pictures could be repeatedly juggled into fresh patterns, that was the bard's art. Ultimately every society, even the industrialised nations which had made bards redundant, derived their culture from that source. In the fragile society of the upriver Iban, Danggang's genius remained as extraordinary as those who once told stories of Beowulf and Cu Cuchulainn, but here in a plastic hotel lobby he became no more than a toothless, illiterate peasant in an absurd hat.

I disliked myself for being able to see him like that. We went to eat at a restaurant in the market-place popular with Iban on *bejalai*. On this middle ground, with mounds of rice, spiced chicken and tapioca leaves crowding out bottles of beer, we all relaxed a little though I still felt uncomfortable. And when I left them to return to the hotel, I disliked myself still more for the pleasure I felt shivering in the air conditioning, bouncing on a soft bed, reading a glossy magazine, and sipping a glass of whisky.

Nevertheless, the sight of Danggang in the lobby had made it clear why the fuss about clothes was so dangerous. If the only authentic Iban wore loin-cloths or short skirts and nothing from the waist up, that society was already wiped out. And in that case, Danggang was indeed no more than an illiterate peasant, and all that was stored within the folds of his unending memory was irrelevant.

I re-filled my glass. It was vital to make Time-Life see how misguided they were in their approach. They might not be able to see it in the pictures, but they must recognise that it existed in the word and the imagination. I took one more drink of whisky and dialled London.

The line was bad. An electric storm, made eerie by its silence, lit the sky outside with a diffused white light which periodically brightened into jagged branches of lightning. Through crackles and cut-off sentences, I shouted down the line the one crucial question, 'What did you think of Tony's first batch of photographs?'

There was a long buzz, then the dying cadence of Gillian Boucher's voice.

'What was that?' I said.

She resorted to telegraphese. ' ... worries. ...lity terrific. Repeat. No ... Quality terrific.' As though the line itself was relieved of tension, her voice abruptly became clear. 'Tell Tony not to worry. The T-shirts weren't obvious. If the ones we've seen were the worst, there's no problem.'

No problem with the 'I'm all yours' in iridescent pink across a *diamanté* heart? No problem with the 'My parents went to Kuching and all they brought back was this lousy T-shirt'? An upsurge of joy enveloped me, and was followed at once by the clutch of remorse. We had got everything out of proportion. Of course Lou was not interested in the number of breasts on display. It was reality he wanted. And it was the reality we would show. At last we understood the auguries.

9

Old Age and Death

THERE WAS AN adolescent exhilaration in Limbang's grin when he said goodbye which would have been unimaginable in the tired face I had seen on our first encounter. With a US$550 traveller's cheque from Time-Life, ostensibly as compensation for looking after us, in actuality to buy a chain-saw, he would have the essential equipment to start his new longhouse, and he could not wait to get going.

On my side, relief at the news from London made me eager to hurry back to the Bangkit, and so our farewells in the street outside the hotel were warm but brief. Danggang maintained an ironic detachment, Ngali the frail formality of age, and Inyang a quick smile; Ading was going with them, but we were due to meet again on the Batang Ai.

By afternoon I had completed an immense shopping list – everything from anti-acid indigestion pills, toothpaste and batteries to fishing-nets, sarongs, axes and sacks of rice – and with the help of a small company of assistants had it aboard the Rejang ferry. On the quay, I looked in vain for Charles Brooke's by-blow, but his absence was too small a disappointment to dent my mood. Under cover of the engines' howl and the crash of water, I sang every verse of 'Blow away the morning dew' at the top of my voice.

Further evidence of the rejuvenating effect of upriver life was apparent when I saw James's stocky figure on the jetty at Song.

145

After ten days with his family he bounced rather than walked, and the contagion of his high spirits was irresistible. We loaded the mountain of supplies into a hired prau, and then celebrated Time-Life's verdict on the photographs in beer cold enough to make the modern world desirable. He had been hunting on the Balleh river, another of the Rejang's tributaries, and his stories of the need for good auguries contained an ambivalence of belief and scepticism which I found congenial.

On one hunt, a friend had threatened to eat a kingfisher if its favourable call proved false but, he called out to the bird, 'If we should be successful, I shall continue to believe you are the ruler of men.'

'And what happened?' I demanded.

'Well of course we were successful,' James grinned. 'A barking-deer appeared soon afterwards, and I shot it.'

Far from wanting to resolve the anomalies of traditional beliefs and modern practices, he delighted in them.

'Did you know that police regulations allow a day's leave to a constable who has a bad dream?' he exclaimed. 'By heck they do, the Assistant Police Superintendent at Kapit told me so himself. And they listen for good birds when they're solving a crime. It works very well, they're a most efficient force.'

After weeks of dry weather, the Bangkit had sunk to become a series of pools joined by rock-strewn shallows. A dozen times an hour, we had to jump out and haul the heavy prau up the rapids. It was like a tug-of-war with banana-skins for footing, and an eight-hour journey took two days. Mocking our efforts, branches thirty feet above us were festooned with rubbish – roots, dead creepers and even a green fishing-net – deposited when the river was in flood.

This spectacular event had occurred two years earlier. Every-one remembered it well, both on the Batang Ai and on the Bangkit. A cloudburst had dumped its load for over eight hours until the rivers were thundering brown torrents. In Ngali's long-house, the water had risen to lap the platform, thirty-five feet

eating your offering. From this earth you will have a magnificent harvest. From this earth you will grow prosperous.'

The words sounded incongruous, but the sight of his solemn face shining with sweat and tension compelled some suspension of disbelief. Then Sebang spoke, and a chill of genuine apprehension struck. 'Look,' she said in a quiet voice, 'someone's attending our feast'.

She appeared to be gazing into the jungle, but her eyes were focused on something much closer. For a moment I feared that she was having a vision, then a finger-thick, diamond-patterned snake detached itself from a branch just to her left, and began to weave its blunt head back and forth. Sebang did not flinch, but Langga at once began to pray again, calling with the triple 'Howa' on Singalang Burong this time.

'Who is calling?' asked Singalang Burong, using Langga's voice.

'I am Langga, the headman of Rumah Langga. I want you to attend my offering.'

'Yes, certainly we'll come,' said Singalang Burong. 'I have sent my son-in-law, he is on your left.' (This was the snake.) 'I have also sent two messengers, and as a result you will gain great wealth and you will be known throughout the land.'

So far as I was concerned that clinched it. There could be no better proof of the rightness of things than the transformation of two pink-faced, sweaty Europeans into messengers of Singalang Burong. Langga felt the same way. Until then, he had suffered our presence. We were something out of the ordinary, but whether a signal of good or bad luck he had not been able to tell. But this sign was unmistakably propitious. The snake had slithered towards the omen sticks, which contained the cool, fertile trills of the Sharma bird, and the whetstones, which would mark the boundaries of the farm. Clearly the gods were smiling, and all the other out-of-the-ordinary happenings could be seen as signs of their favour.

It was the unexpectedness of the snake's visit rather than the snake itself which made the moment auspicious, and so when it crawled sluggishly into the stump of the dead tree, and threatened to disrupt the rest of the proceedings, Sebang told her husband to chase it away.

'No,' said Langga decidedly, 'we should leave it.'

Since he was only talking in his role as husband, Sebang decided to ignore his advice, and in her role as wife drew her bush-knife and chopped away at the stump until the snake slithered off into the grass. Langga affected not to notice.

There were other offerings of rice to the gods of the earth, wind, moon, stars and sun; a hen was sacrificed and the first small saplings were felled with a bush-knife ceremonially sharpened with sacred whetstones. It was a remarkable ceremony, but the son-in-law of Singalang Burong had given it an extra quality. Langga was not a demonstrative man, but after this his attitude warmed to something near effusiveness. When clearing began in earnest, he made it plain that our presence was positively welcomed, and he did not even object when James and I armed ourselves with axes. So far as I was concerned, that was the ultimate proof of my new standing.

Once the trees were felled, the concern of the longhouse turned to the weather. What they needed was a long, dry spell so that the dead trees and undergrowth would blaze up when they put a torch to it. In some years the rain came down relentlessly, and when they could delay no longer, the wood hardly took fire, and only the branches were reduced to ash. When that happened the planting had to be done through a trellis of scorched trees. Pests like grasshoppers and beetles flourished, and disease was common. A good burn on the other hand produced a blackened hillside scattered with charred trunks. Few farmers would recognise it as a field suitable for cultivation, but for the Iban it was ideal.

The average farm was about four acres, but Langga's site was nearer five. This was about the maximum size that a family could handle. Any larger, and it would be impossible to keep the weeds down and to guard against the pigs, deer and monkeys which always raided the growing crop. Given the twelve-year cycle needed for forest regeneration, each family required access to around fifty or sixty acres of land. It was not an impossible demand, and there was undoubtedly enough jungle in Sarawak to satisfy it.

It would be too much to say that peace and brotherhood now reigned in the Time-Life team, but we were able to discuss with only intermittently gritted teeth the choice of a subject for 'A Day in the Life'. Sebang was alas ruled out because she figured so prominently in the *manggol* rites, but I made a strong case for selecting instead Matu, the river's most single-minded and successful philanderer, and as such certain to be a source of first-class copy. In his newly dominant mood, Tony swept this aside.

'I think we'll do Tigang,' he said.

Tigang was one of the oldest men in the longhouse, and the last still to tie his hair back in an old-fashioned pigtail. The modern world had scarcely touched him. All his life had been spent in the forest, sometimes living on tributaries of the Rejang, at others settling far across the border in Kalimantan. He was not going to make good copy, but he looked fine. His shoulders and legs were heavily tattooed, his hair was white, and he spent much of the day making fish-traps in the form of long, conical baskets. At night he slept fully dressed, in a tracksuit acquired on *bejalai*, lying on a bedroll in a corner of the kitchen where the ashes in the hearth provided heat for his septuagenarian bones. When he awoke, he lay on his back staring at the beams and the shingled ceiling. He could hear the rush of the river down the rapids and the harsh cry of the fighting cocks passing along the gallery. Long before dawn, his wife and niece stole silently into the room to build up the fire and start heating the water. I knew all this, because even longer before dawn, Tony had woken me so that we could sit in the kitchen and observe each moment of Tigang's day.

He was a solitary man who had married late and come to join his wife's family. It was twenty years since he had arrived, and he had grown too old to chop trees or hunt pig, but he still had to get enough food for himself. The only pensioners in the longhouse were the old woman Saul who was bedridden and lived on a few handfuls of rice, and a simple-minded woman in her forties who looked after the hens.

Tigang's speciality was fishing. Every morning he inspected the traps he had set the night before, then set about repairing them or making new ones, and every evening he set them in place again. Woodsmoke from the fire made him cough. It was warm now in the kitchen. Clearly he did not look forward to the damp air and cold water outside, for when his wife pulled away his mosquito net, he grumbled inarticulately at her, and for a few more minutes lay where he was. Then he turned his head towards the centre of the room and lazily opened his eyes.

The look of horror on his face was pitiable. His mouth opened wide, his face muscles went rigid, and his eyes bulged from between stretched lids. Just a couple of yards from his bed sat two white *antu* with faces covered in hair, one festooned with cameras, the other scribbling in a notebook. He clenched his eyes tight shut and leant back on his bedroll as though he hoped the vision would go away.

Presumably, while he lay there, the memory of the arrangement he had made with us the night before seeped back into his mind, for his face relaxed and he stole another less amazed look at us. Soon afterwards he got decisively to his feet and began to follow the routine of every day. We followed behind him as though we were *papparazzi* after a film star.

What Tigang thought of our behaviour it was impossible to imagine. We had attempted to explain about the 'A Day in the Life of ...' section, but he could hardly have guessed that he would be dogged every moment of the day. Through the grey mist of pre-dawn, we trailed him along twisting paths, and not until we had flushed out three other males from the longhouse, including Sibat and Langga, who had squatted down behind the bushes for a morning pee, did we realise his intention.

This was deeply embarrassing, for almost the only condition that had been imposed upon us was that we should not try to photograph the private parts of anyone in the longhouse.

Modesty about displaying themselves compelled even the men to squat when they urinated, and the place by the river where they defecated had to be strictly avoided while anyone was there. Now here we were apparently trying to photograph poor Tigang in the act. We scuttled back to the longhouse in confusion.

This lavatorial misapprehension was mutual. They considered our habit of defecating in the forest as less hygienic than doing it in the river. However, the mighty pile of pink lavatory paper which we had brought with us did, I think, raise some doubts in their minds about whether we performed exactly the same act as they when we scurried off with a toilet roll in our hands.

Apart from calls of nature, his and ours, we never left Tigang. He was a subject that brought out the best in Tony. Before the day was done, he had shot around twenty rolls of film – Tigang wading out to his trap, Tigang lifting out his empty trap, Tigang examining his empty trap, Tigang putting his empty trap back in place, Tigang wading despondently back to his prau. Such enthusiasm was wonderful to see.

The despair of the early days had disappeared with much of the fat, and it was finally possible to understand how he had earned his reputation. He missed nothing, and as a good photographer should, he bracketed most shots with others at slightly different apertures to get the right exposure. Ayum watched with a bemused grin. He had seen Tony at work for over a month, and still could not get used to what he did.

'A sensible person would never live like that,' he finally declared when he got back to Batang Ai. 'Only a madman would go around photographing every second, every moment of the day. Anything he saw, Tony would photograph.' He tried to think of the most unlikely subject imaginable. 'He would even have photographed a bitch giving birth.' It was true, he would have shot a roll, but when Lou said he did not want to rob dogs from the main story, you shot them till their paws stopped twitching.

His exploration of the bushes was almost the last moment of leisure that Tigang had except for eating – and I noticed that

153

even the elderly put away more rice than I did. Thereafter the process of manufacturing a fish-trap occupied him. It began with cutting thin strips from a long bamboo cane. Beside him, his wife Jatai sat weaving a plain basket, and looking up the gallery it was apparent that by 7.30 in the morning everyone, with the exception of young children, was occupied at some task. Most of the adults were out on the river or at their farm-sites, but Limau who lived on the other side of Langga was mending a mat; Munoh, the witch-like mother of Jingga was splitting rattan; and Ugau, from the lowest and poorest apartment, was stripping down his recalcitrant outboard (more in hope than expectation, until Tony helpfully pointed out that the leads were crossed). This purposeful activity happened continuously and almost casually. Ilun, a middle-aged man with gold teeth who lived at the top end of the longhouse, suspended a long net from a beam and began knotting lead weights to its border while he talked to his wife who sat weaving a straw basket. Next to them a group of women appeared to be gossiping by the open doorway to the platform, but from closer range I saw one was picking grit from a heap of rice, another comforting a sick baby, a third wielding a long stick to keep hens away from some rice drying on the platform outside, a fourth working on a small loom, and a fifth twisting cord for her. When one activity ceased another began. The basket was later put away and a jar brought out for cleaning, the loom was laid aside and a bush-knife taken out to be sharpened. Once the rice had been cleaned, the chickens were fed, and when the baby fell asleep, the washing was retrieved from a boulder where it had been drying in the sun. There was no division between work and leisure, every form of activity contributed to the sustenance of life.

Nothing distracted Tigang from the fish-traps until Ilun hung up his fishing-net, and came past with a bush-knife to collect some coconuts off his trees. He paused to ask Tigang how the fishing had gone, and Tigang, slightly on his mettle, blamed the absence of fish in his trap, not on a bad bird, but on the moon.

'The best time is at the full moon during the dry season,' he declared. 'I've sometimes found the trap seething with fish at that time of year, it's when the fish spawn.'

Ilun shook his head. 'It's not just the fish spawning that happens at the full moon,' he said warningly, 'that's when the spirits go out hunting humans.'

Tigang grunted, evidently feeling that this was irrelevant. 'I threw my net over the trap,' he went on, 'and came up with twenty pounds of catfish.'

Ilun smiled politely as fishermen's audiences do, and went off to cut down three huge green coconuts growing close to the platform. Tigang returned to the task of binding strips of bamboo to a circular frame made of rattan creeper. In shape it formed a funnel which narrowed to a waist then opened slightly to a long chamber which would hold the bait and the fish. By three o'clock it was complete, and he had only allowed himself two short breaks. One was lunch, but the other was provided by the arrival of a prau carrying seven women. Instead of coming to the longhouse's side of the river, they tied up on the far bank, and began to climb a path over the hill. A dull gleam came into Tigang's eye at the sight of their slender bodies. He put down the trap and walked out to the platform.

'Where are you going to?' he shouted.

The girl in the lead cried out that they were going to the Iyat, a river on the other side of the hill. Before Tigang could reply, he was joined by Matu.

'Can I come with you?' he yelled.

'Sure,' shouted the entire group.

Matu grinned. He was Limau's son, and his reputation as a womaniser was known from the source of the Bangkit to its mouth.

'You would have to carry me,' he said.

'OK, I'll do that,' the last girl in the line called out.

'But not on your back,' leered Matu, 'you would have to carry me on your front.'

There was a moment's silence while the implications were worked out, then shrieks of laughter rang through the valley.

Tigang smiled a little ruefully, and returned to an old man's concerns.

His day did not finish when the trap was made. Again we got into the prau and followed him as he poled upriver to the second rapid above the longhouse. There he hauled rocks into position to form an arrow-shape pointing upstream, and at its tip he placed his trap. The weight of the stones made his spine and ribs bend alarmingly, and the bones pressed so hard against the stretched skin that when he straightened his back their imprint could still be seen. Even after he had drifted back in his prau and washed himself in the river, he had still to collect the hens into their coops, which were suspended on lines from the floor of the gallery, and haul them up off the ground out of reach of snakes and other predators. By six o'clock, when he had eaten some more rice and fish, he could only loll against the wall wrapped in a sarong and tracksuit top, incapable of any movement more strenuous than chewing betel. There we finally left him, just in time to see Matu in a brilliant yellow T-shirt deftly pole a prau downstream to *ngayap* or woo the girls in the next longhouse downriver.

'Now why didn't we choose him?' I asked enviously. 'Matu's daily life would be worth a book on its own.'

Nevertheless, Tony's choice was the right one. Sex was always interesting, but as Aching's behaviour had suggested, and I was shortly to find out for myself, it did not carry the same psychological significance for the Iban as it did in the West. On the other hand, as might have been expected of a people who took heads to promote the fertility of their rice farms and their women, death was of such importance that they could hardly contemplate it.

'The whole purpose of Iban religion is the denial of death,' James said when I asked him about it. 'It refuses to accept that it happens. The soul leaves the body and continues to live in the spirit world, and its life there is a continuation of the one here. Nothing ends.'

It was only a matter of days after we arrived in the longhouse that Munoh, Jingga's mother, fell ill. Until then she had been amongst the most active of the old women. On most mornings she fed the hens and supervised the children with fierce authority. In the household she wielded the influence of a constitutional monarch, giving a raven's croak of approval to matters she agreed with, and maintaining an impatient silence about the rest. Her opinion was rarely asked but always obvious, and nothing escaped her attention.

When she fell sick just before the festival began, Jingga was distraught, and the entire apartment became submerged in gloom. Suddenly frail and small, she was laid out on a mattress in the living-room, and an offering was made for her recovery. There was no improvement, and in the course of a night and a day she declined fast. On the second night, Michael was asked to help, and he gave antibiotics and a laxative. While he waited in the darkened room to see whether these would work, Engkin, a man of about thirty from the upriver end of the longhouse, came and stood beside Munoh. He began to chant over her and pressed charms to her head and stomach. Suddenly, in a movement which took Michael by surprise, he breathed out a great sheet of flame whose momentary glare lit the apartment and illuminated the corpse-like face of the old woman.

The next day Monoh was on her feet, a little shaken but as quick as ever to rasp at the children. Her subsequent eagerness to marry Michael off to her granddaughter might have sprung from a sense of gratitude, but more probably she attributed her recovery to Engkin's charms and fire-eating.

Engkin was one of two *manang* or healers in the longhouse. He was a good-humoured, practical man, but something of a disappointment to Time-Life. He was due to be the subject of a mini-essay, which was admittedly less crucial than a picture theme, but nonetheless important. 'Traditionally,' my briefing paper assured me, 'the *manang* should be a hermaphrodite, and many of the Iban shamans are blind or handicapped.' According to Erik Jensen's authoritative study, *The Iban and their Religion*, blindness was an asset in the spirit world, which was their area

157

of expertise, because most activity there took place at night when the normally sighted were at a disadvantage. Instead of being a blind hermaphrodite, Engkin was a clear-sighted, competent farmer and efficient hunter, whose only quirk was to dislike the taste of wild pig. In Time-Life terms, he was the equivalent of a T-shirt. All the same he was genuine.

The spirit in his dream had taught him the fire-eating technique and had directed him where to find his charms, most of which were unusually shaped stones and pieces of polished wood. In addition, he had a larger piece of quartz which he used as a kind of telescope or crystal ball to see into the spirit world.

The rites he performed varied, but all of them concerned the state of the patient's *semengat* or soul. This inhabited the body and specifically the head, but in times of illness it wandered abroad, occasionally of its own accord but more frequently because an evil spirit had tempted it away. In such cases Engkin had to find it, and this was the purpose of the fire-eating act, both to scare away the evil spirit and to act as a beacon to Munoh's soul.

It did not impress Ugau, however. He had been beset by constant setbacks other than his malfunctioning outboard, and the most worrying was his youngest child, a sickly boy with a listless air. Instead of asking Engkin for help, he turned to one of the bards who came for the festival. Presumably, this was because the *ensera* or sacred songs which the bards committed to memory gave them an insight into the spirit world, but perhaps also because the cure he had in mind was oral. During his years in Sabah where he had worked in the oilfields, Ugau had been impressed by the power associated with European names, and he was determined that his sons should benefit. One was therefore called James Bond – 'a very strong name', he explained – and another Andrew after the prince of that name. Unfortunately Andrew remained pallid and ailing, and Ugau had decided that his name must be changed.

Early in the morning, the entire family and the bard went down to the river where a prayer was chanted and a cock sacrificed. The bard dunked Andrew in the river then splashed him with water in a ceremony which was not a christening but a washing away of the old name and all its attributes. For the moment he was nameless, but back in the apartment six dishes of rice had been laid out on the floor, each with a name attached. The bard made an offering, and the family's fighting cock was brought in to peck out a new name for the boy. It edged towards the plates, eyed the one labelled Senang, glanced at the one called Mujap, and finally pecked a grain from the plate marked Daut. I never liked that cock. It was the first to crow in the morning, and it did so with a hoarse, smoker's baritone which produced a sympathetic constriction in my throat, but he was certainly in touch with the cosmos, for with his new name Daut immediately showed signs of improvement.

What the healers' art demonstrated was the union between the spirit world and the physical. They were as closely joined as a body and its shadow, and every movement in one had its counterpart in the other. Their cosmos prompted Freeman to something near eloquence:

'The Iban have an absolute and fervent belief in the immortality of the soul and in the existence of an afterworld, which they call Sabayan. To this shadowy land go the souls of the Iban dead – men, women and children. It is also an unshakeable Iban belief that all objects possess separable soul counterparts, called *semengat*, and the Iban are utterly convinced that any article can be taken to the afterworld in the form of its soul counterpart. Sabayan, indeed, is looked upon as being an almost exact replica of this world, and it is the solemn duty of the living to equip the dead for their future existence. So it is that every dead person is furnished with burial property ...'

This single-eyed view of existence offered comfort against the terror of death, and when this came at the end of a long life one could think that it was almost nothing at all. 'She's come back,' the mourners said when Saul finally died, as though her life had been just an excursion away from home.

Throughout the merriment of the festival, the old woman had

159

lain, hardly stirring, in a small shelter built on to the back of the apartment. The drone of the bard's incantations and the laughter of the guests may just have reached her consciousness, for when they came to an end, she died. She had been facing the hill behind the longhouse, but a last convulsion had twisted her round towards the river, and now she lay tiny and curled up like a foetus, the pale skin stretched taut over her ribs.

She was washed where she lay and her limbs were stretched out. Then she was carried into the kitchen and a clean skirt was put on her. When Engkin had anointed her head and feet with oil she was brought into the gallery, and through the night two relatives from a longhouse downriver kept watch at her head while four women sat by her side, sometimes coming close to wail over her corpse. Early the next morning while the sky was still grey, she was wrapped in a woven rug, which was tied with creeper and suspended from a rice-pounding pole. Led by her grandson, Alo, carrying a flaming torch, a procession carried her body down to the shore. From there a cortège of five boats took her up the rapids and across the long green pool above them.

Opposite the little river leading to Langga's farm, they landed at a beach and an offering was made to the spirits of the dead. Engkin measured her body and poled across the river to the opposite shore where the flood had deposited a pile of grey tree trunks. Selecting a log about thirty inches in diameter he began to chop off a length of five and a half feet. Meanwhile Nyanggau with his uncle, Tigang, and Alo took another boat upriver and crossed over above the little stream where a wooded hill rose steeply. This was the longhouse's graveyard where more than fifty of its inhabitants were buried.

Manju, the other healer, went over to join Engkin, and their blows on the hard wood rang through the forest. Even with two it was slow work, and Nyanggau's voice could soon be heard calling from the graveyard to ask if they were ready. When the length of log was cut through, Engkin towed it back to the beach, where it was split in two and hollowed out with an adze. Still wrapped in the rug, Saul's body was put into her tree-trunk coffin, and the two halves bound together with creeper. Now she was taken over to the graveyard where, followed by men carrying goods that would be left at her grave, she was borne in silence up the steep, uneven path. A dim light filtering through the leaves revealed the graves on either side. They were marked by shelters of corrugated iron or palm leaves set on sapling frames, and beneath each was a litter of household goods – jars, aluminium kettles, a metal chair, a yellow plastic bucket – half-covered in dead leaves.

A pile of yellow earth halfway up the hill marked Saul's grave. Tigang and Alo stood in the hole, each wearing a yoke of forked sticks so that his soul was held in place and could not be taken away by the spirits of the dead who were coming for Saul. At the graveside her coffin was placed in the ground, but in that moment of incongruity which funerals produce the grave was found to be too small. No one said anything and Tigang dug away until the coffin would fit. Then at last Saul's body was lowered to its resting-place and the yellow earth was shovelled over it.

Jingga had carried up a jar, and this was placed on the fresh grave, upside down so that snakes would not curl up inside. Beside it Saul's family put a suitcase of clothes, a kettle, a tray, and a basket containing rice, fish and *tuak*. With the spiritual counterparts of these accompanying her, the dead woman would not be ashamed in Sabayan by lack of clothes or food. Above them was erected a temporary shelter, and then the party yoked their souls firmly to their bodies with forked sticks and returned to the river.

There was now a palpable release of tension, and for the first time people began to talk, pointing out the other graves. The one immediately below Saul's belonged to her son, and below him was the small plot where an infant child of Langga's was buried. Still, it was not until they were out of the dark wood and across the river that they relaxed entirely. Some of the young men had gone fishing while the coffin was being made, and now over a meal of grilled fish and *tuak*, and with the rising sun on their

161

backs, it was a time for elegies – generous elegies because the souls of the newly dead lingered and were apt to misconstrue what was said about them.

'She was a kind woman,' said Jingga.

'It was hard for her,' Engkin pointed out, 'losing her son, and her grandchildren leaving the apartment.'

'But she was kind,' Nyanggau insisted, 'she always thought of others.'

'She was thoughtful in her dying too,' Jingga added. 'It would have been difficult if she had died during the festival.'

'We should have lost time from farming if she had died later,' Sibat said.

'If she had died when we were about to burn,' Ugau commented, 'we would have had to wait another week.'

'It was just the right time to die,' Mandau summed up, 'while the boys were still at home from *bejalai*, and before we had gone back to work.'

'Yes,' Jingga sighed, 'she was kind right enough', and with that they finished off their meal and drifted downriver back to the longhouse.

10

Superstitious Terrors

SAUL'S DEATH CREATED a sober atmosphere in the longhouse. Although only her family were required to observe the full mourning prohibitions against wearing jewellery, having sexual intercourse, and working, the other members of the community did not leave the house for two days and observed a sort of wet Sunday restraint on their behaviour. This was partly out of respect for Saul and her family, but largely out of a genuine fear of bothering her ghost which was still lurking round the longhouse.

The Iban were so rumbustious and matter of fact in their relationship with their gods and their messengers, that their fear of spirits took me by surprise. In childhood it was fostered readily enough, but it also haunted adults just as keenly. When Michael and I returned from a visit to the graveyard at Rumah Langga, Limau came up and asked whether we had seen any ghosts. She was such a jolly, coarse-tongued woman, and so disrespectful of authority, that I thought she must be joking, and replied that of course we had. 'What's more,' I added, 'they made a sound like this', and blew through cupped hands to make an owl-like hoot. Poor Limau's face crumpled with terror; she clapped her hands over her ears and rushed off into her apartment. After nightfall, even the adults tried not to find themselves alone in an apartment, and the children were unnaturally well-behaved.

For most of the nineteenth century, Iban society was dominated by the belief that only the ineffably potent fertility of a skull could compensate for death's desolation. When Saul was born, the mourning period for important people lasted a year, and in theory the taking of a head was still necessary to bring it to an end. In practice, however, a ritual hunt for game had been increasingly adopted since the Brookes began to put a brake on head-hunting. The hunt was designed to provide the bereaved family with food, but more importantly it offered a symbol of solidarity with them. It was one of the few projects which involved the whole community, and like any communal enterprise a meeting had to be held to decide when it should take place and what form it should adopt. The meeting at Rumah Langga was typically robust.

There was considerable debate about the number of people who should go, and which boats would be needed. 'If the white people want to come,' Ilun claimed, 'we'll have to take the big boats to fit their arses in.' The white people certainly did want to come. There had been a lot of hunting, and I had interviewed a lot of hunters, but so far I had never seen an Iban with spear in hand and dogs at heel bring down a wild boar. It was not just a photo-essay, it could make an entire chapter.

It took some time to rein in the freewheeling debate on the size of white arses, and decide that five boats would be needed, of which one should be large. Then Langga asked where the expedition should go and how long it should stay out. Everyone was in favour of going far upriver, beyond Membuas's longhouse, but the real problem lay in deciding how long they should stay away. Everyone knew that they should be out clearing land for the rice harvest, but most of them also wanted to make the most of a genuine excuse to undertake the much more enjoyable duty of hunting. With his customary shrewdness, Langga attempted to draw the debate to a close by suggesting a compromise of staying out one night. There seemed to be a general agreement to this proposal when Mangan, who made a point of contributing to meetings which the men thought they were running, yelled from her customary place on the fringe of the circle, 'Why bother to stay a night if you can get enough food in a day?'

In an irritated tone Langga pointed out that the best time to get pig was in the evening waiting by one of their watering holes – that was why they would have to stay away at least one night.

'I remember when I waited till night by a watering-hole for pig,' Jingga began, and with a stir of anticipation and resignation, the meeting settled back while he told the interminable story of his hunt. With much eye-rolling he described the terrors of the gathering darkness, and when the pig finally came he gripped his thigh to indicate the size of its hams, and finally with a weighty shake of his head he revealed how in the gloom he had missed it from point-blank range. He shifted his betel from one cheek to the other. 'Night-time is the wrong time to get pig at a waterhole,' he concluded.

Most people listened with evident enjoyment to a story which all must have heard before, but Langga sat with a stony face. He did not attempt to let the point be debated.

'Of course you get pig at night,' he burst out. 'If a man has a good gun, and if he shoots straight, he will kill them. He must shoot straight, that's all.'

The reproach to Jingga's uncertain aim was clear enough, and he bowed his grey head to hide the fact that he was hurt by it. Their exchange was part of an undertow of rivalry between the two which was just detectable at the festival, but had become more marked since I had returned from Sibu.

When James reappeared, Langga claimed the privileges of blood ties and promptly installed him on his strip of gallery. The significance of this move was not lost on Jingga's apartment. Among the supplies I had brought back for the longhouse was one bag of rice to be shared equally between the families that looked after us.

'When the food is divided, you will see that the headman gets more than anyone else,' Bulik predicted, and was quickly proved right.

165

On the strength of having James as his guest, however fleet-ingly, Langga awarded himself two shares. Resentment simmered in Jingga's apartment. Although Langga was respected, he was never as popular as his elder brother, and his hard com-petitiveness struck many as greed. This latest act of acquisi-tiveness prompted Jingga to make a further attempt to persuade Michael of his duties. It was made more urgent because he in his turn was planning to go to Kuching for a few days. On the eve of his departure Jingga summoned him to a family meeting.

It was an impressive occasion. Munoh sat in her usual place behind the door, her withered breasts hanging to her lap, and the toothless pucker of her lips forming a moustache-shaped shadow; next to her Dambak, looking more than ever like a Quaker woman with her hair scraped back and her upper lip pulled down at the corners; then Jingga, his brow carved into tragic furrows; Bulik, sleekly grinning; and finally Orin, scraping paint off her nails with a knife, her perfect face on its slender neck touched by a slightly plaintive expression.

Jingga began by suggesting that the family, including Michael whom he addressed as *anak* or 'son', might like to make a visit to see a rock some way downriver which was coloured by a copper deposit. No one said anything to this, so abandoning conventional politeness, Jingga edged nearer to his chief concern.

'Aching must come back here,' he said. 'It is not right that she should leave her home. I shall bring her back.'

Again Michael said nothing. His left foot exercised a magnetic effect on his eyes.

Jingga sighed and tried again. Michael had told him of an anthropology project which might take him to Kapit, he pointed out. That was close enough for Jingga to visit. And he would do so. Frequently. The pauses between his words grew longer, for by now he had reached the heart of the matter. Michael's gaze never left his foot.

'I will never ask you for money,' Jingga declared defiantly. There was no comment. 'But you have lived with the Iban,' he went on, 'you know they are poor, and often need help –

especially money, and because you are generous, you always give help – and money.'

My heart went out to him. In an argument, the least he could expect was to hear a reply to his eloquence, but here his words fell into a void. His head sank with the knowledge of defeat, and his belly sagged further over his black bathing pants.

'You will give money,' he said hopelessly, 'but I, Jingga, shall never ask for it.' He looked at his feet, Michael looked at his feet, Orin scraped her nails, and no one said anything for a long time. Then Jingga said, 'I must go for a shit', and left.

My sympathies were with Jingga, but so I suspected were Michael's. We went out on to the gallery where he unburdened himself. It was Sulang who troubled him most.

'I can hear him crying at night,' he said wearily. 'It has an unbearable, stabbing quality which reminds me of my first night away from home at boarding-school, sobbing myself to sleep. But I wasn't two years old.'

For the first and only time I had an inkling of what lay behind his thesis, and why he valued so highly the support and affection which most Iban children received in abundance. It shed a very different light upon him, and I found that I was genuinely sorry when he left for Kuching the next morning.

His departure meant that he missed the ritual hunting trip. To my baffled fury, so did I. Ever since he had been told of Time-Life's reaction to his photographs, Tony had shown himself determined to let nothing stand in his way in producing the definitive photographic record of life in an Iban longhouse. After the meeting about the hunt, he took me aside.

'I don't think you should come on this hunting trip,' he said weightily. 'You would just be in the way.'

'And how the hell am I supposed to write about Langga's eyeball to eyeball confrontation with a wild boar if I'm not there?' I demanded.

'I'll tell you about anything interesting that happens,' he assured me. 'Remember what Lou said about the pictures – they're the important thing. And on the hunt, there's going to be so much happening, I can't afford to keep looking out for white limbs in the frame.'

I glared at him for fully ten seconds. The hunt, my hunt, had been taken away. There would be no Wart and Kay reenactment, no technicoloured descriptions. I was speechless with anger.

'Anyway, I'll probably only be taking context shots,' he said consolingly.

'I have no idea what a context shot is supposed to be,' I said huffily, 'and I don't have the slightest wish to know because I'm not coming.'

To no one's real surprise, Langga's mother had a dream that night which was about as bad as it could be. There were three moons in the sky, of which the central one was burning red, and a voice said, 'This longhouse is hot.' This meant hot in an emotional and spiritual sense, and if the temperature was not brought down quickly it could have dangerous consequencs. At an anxious conference the next morning, it was agreed that the longhouse needed to be cooled as soon as possible, but that this could not be done until the mourning period for Saul came to an end. The expedition, therefore, set off without delay.

After a night and almost two days' absence, the whooping cry of a head-hunter from the bottom of the ladder announced the hunting party's return. Jingga and I asked with equal interest for news of their success. The fishing had gone well, and Bulik came up the ladder with almost thirty pounds of fish. Then Langga appeared with his shotgun slung over his shoulder.

'A bad bird,' he announced unconcernedly. 'The hunting was not good.'

Not good? 'What happened?' I asked Tony when he finally struggled up the ladder with his heavy camera bag. He looked at me irritatedly.

'We saw a pig on the bank and Langga missed with both barrels at close range,' he said. 'Then we saw two Argus pheasants and he shot at one and missed it as well. Then he fired again, and finally got it with the second barrel.' He stumped

darkness, drunk and happy, I felt myself tumbling inwards, reduced to insignificance beneath the vast shimmer of stars overhead and the endless blackness of the forest. Instead of terror, it felt as though the boundaries had shifted to a more comfortable position. Previously when I had watched the Iban huddled round the lamps, I had been struck by their fragility, and by the darkness pressing in on them, but now when I looked through the open doorway their shining bodies seemed to be an integral part of the night. They were one with their world, and where it ended so did they.

I went back to my place opposite Membuas, dizzier than ever. He pushed a full bowl to me. His own was empty. *Tuak* left an ache in the stomach, and my head was swimming. This bowl had to be finished off in one or not at all. I poured it down, choking on its sweetened bitterness. For several minutes, I sat there swaying and somnolent. It was enough. An honourable draw. I lifted my head to focus on Membuas. He looked terrible. His brow had contracted into two great lumps over his eyes, and these were pink and brown and squinting.

'Offer him another bowl now,' James urged me. 'Don't wait. Challenge him now.'

Only the whiff of his competitiveness impelled me to fill up the bowls once more. Without pausing to let myself think how I felt, I lifted mine to my lips, opened wide, and swallowed. The *tuak* poured into my mouth and overflowed down my cheeks. I swallowed and swallowed, and eventually the milky river dried up, and I could turn the bowl over to show it was empty. Membuas stared heavily at his brimming bowl, then leant forward and touched it with his fingers to show its spirit that he meant no disrespect in refusing it. With considerable difficulty he got to his feet and lurched out to the platform. The sound of his vomiting roused the pigs and brought them scrunching and oinking to the unexpected feast.

The outcome of this evening was twofold. The more obvious was that Membuas challenged me to a rematch. The other was the sense of having glimpsed for a moment what it meant to live

in a unitary world. However nonsensical it was to claim that a
woodpecker was god's son-in-law, it enabled a person to think
like the jungle, listening to its messages rather than his thoughts.

The advantages of this way of thinking did not immediately
appear obvious. Although mourning had ended, no work could
be done until the longhouse had been cooled. Mandau got up at
dawn after the ritual feast to collect the liquid notes of the White-
rumped Sharma in some omen sticks, but as he was about to set
out he heard the wheezing cough of a barking deer from the far
bank. This too was a bad omen, and so for another day the
longhouse was confined to barracks. Nothing had changed since
Charles Brooke had observed:

'What with bad omens, sounds, signs, adverse dreams, and
deaths, two thirds of their time is not spent in farm labour.
When they have a plentiful harvest, the greater part of the
stock is used for giving different kinds of feasts. This is of course
a dead waste and for the remainder of the year the inhabitants
are badly off ... Many a time have strange visitors remarked
what happy people the Dyaks must be, who farm and gain a
livelihood with so little trouble, and are not pestered by irritating social conventionalities. But this is not true by any
means.'

Denied access to their farms, almost everyone became busier
than ever inside the longhouse. Some caught up on the routine
of pounding rice and sharpening knives. Jingga and Bulik
repaired their harpoon guns, and Dambak began to weave some
red-dyed rattan into a decorative mat. Only Matu and Sibat took
a complete rest, and spent most of their morning setting up
sparring contests between their fighting cocks. Infected by so
much activity, Tony completed a portfolio of photographs of the
apartments, I wrote character sketches of their inhabitants, and
James generously interviewed the women and children on my
behalf.

When he gave me his completed questionnaire, I saw that
amongst other things, he had asked a group of the women who
had entertained us the day before what they thought of me.

172

Limau, whom I had terrified with my graveyard hooting, had answered for all of them, 'He could be an Iban – except for the colour of his skin.'

No flattery is more potent than to be told that you are what you secretly dream of being. For days I preened myself. I knew it was no more than politeness. I knew she should also have added, 'except for his ignorance of the language, the culture and the country', but I did not care. It felt like acceptance, and I was delighted.

As though to endorse my happiness, the fruit season arrived, and for a few weeks we lived in a gourmet's paradise. The first fruit was *sibau*, which looked like a red conker, but when split open revealed a flesh resembling lychee. As with everything else in her well-organised household, Mangan's fruit trees ripened first, and she used to tip a basket of them on to the mat in the gallery for everyone to eat. Hers were large and juicy, but Nyanggau's wife used to collect the fruit from trees growing wild in the jungle, which were smaller and had the sweetness of wild strawberries. Then for variety came *linsap*, a yellow citrus fruit with a sharp tang to it, then black-skinned mangostines whose rosy flesh had a sour-sweet flavour, then *mwang*, which were scented and tasted like mangoes.

By the basketload they arrived, fruits I had never seen before, and whose names I never learned. In the face of such a glut, self-restraint and moderation were bad manners, and by a miraculous dispensation they could be eaten till you were tired of eating, and there were no ill effects.

Despite their enthusiasm for these fruit, the pleasure of the longhouse's inhabitants seemed a little muted, as though they were reserving their full enthusiasm for something even better. Early in July it came. Ayum spotted some from a prau as he was descending a rapid, and rammed in his pole to bring the boat to a stop in mid-flow so that he could jump out to collect them. About the size of a pineapple, but with a green, spiky skin, it grew on a tree more than eighty feet high, and the thump as it hit the ground was enough to make adults and children drop whatever they were doing and race out looking for it. Then with a sharp blow from a bush-knife they split it open to reveal a creamy white flesh. This was the durian fruit.

In the nineteenth century, A. R. Wallace, co-founder with Darwin of the theory of evolution, visited Borneo and Malaya in search of evidence for his ideas, but finding himself distracted by his passion for durian, he devoted valuable time to analysing its bewitching taste:

'The pulp is the eatable part, and its consistence and flavour are indescribable. A rich, butterlike custard, highly flavoured with almonds gives the best general idea of it, but intermingled with this come wafts of flavour that call to mind cream-cheese, onion sauce, brown sherry and other incongruities. Then there is the rich glutinous smoothness in the pulp which nothing else possesses but which adds to its delicacy. It is neither acid, nor sweet, nor juicy, yet one feels the want of none of these qualities for it is perfect as it is. It produces no nausea or other bad effect, and the more you eat of it the less you feel inclined to stop.'

It was in short the perfect fruit, or would have been had it not possessed the further incongruity of smelling like kerosene. For this reason, it was usually eaten on the gallery, but on one glorious day, when Langga returned after a morning in the forest, Sebang provided half a dozen durian for lunch, then followed them with grilled *suma* fish – about the size and flavour of brown trout – accompanied by bamboo shoots and breadfruit. At the end Langga produced a plate piled with slabs of wild honey. It was the sort of meal you would only get in paradise.

So imbued had I become with the Iban idea that when James suggested that we put a net out on the river, I chose a narrow prau and managed to take the craft down the rapids, standing upright with scarcely a spasm. I persuaded Ayum to show me how to throw a fishing-net, looping it in folds over both arms, then with a discus thrower's swivel of the hips from the back foot to the front hurling it forward in a broad arc. The next time I went to help Langga clear trees from his land, I decided to go barefoot through the forest as the Iban did. Langga's son had taken the dogs, and in the middle of the morning they began to bark from deep inside the untouched jungle. James did not hesitate.

'*Babu* – pig,' he shouted, and dropping his axe hurtled off into the trees. I followed, at first gingerly, and then as the barking rose to an hysterical descant at a flat-out gallop, under the creepers, round the stumps, down tunnels of thorn, and up muddy hills. When finally we came up with the dogs, they were gazing foolishly at a hole in the ground, and whatever had made its home there, it was no pig. My legs were scored and bleeding, and leeches clustered on my ankles and forearms, but without shoes to blind them, my feet had found their way unscathed through the spikes and thorns. For one panting moment, I felt that I had broken into the Iban world. I could not think of any advantages in the Western way of life, nor of any disadvantages in the Sarawak forest.

11

Sweethearts and Sweet Talk

'I WANT CHOICE, give me plenty of choice,' Lou had said. 'Don't stop with a day in the life of a hunter or whatever, shoot a woman's day, a kid's.' Herod would have talked like Lou. 'Shoot a beautiful child,' he said.

And so from Tigang, we went to Pantai, who was as slender as a bamboo frond, and beautiful enough to go on a chocolate box. Nevertheless, at twelve years old, she was already performing most of the duties expected of a grown woman. When her parents left for work on the farm, her father, Sibat, felt it necessary to explain about feeding the pigs that rootled about in the slime beneath the longhouse – 'Don't be afraid of them, and make sure the smallest one gets it share' – but rightly assumed that she needed no advice about sweeping the apartment clean, washing clothes down at the river, or fetching water to cook the evening meal which her parents expected to find waiting for them on their return.

That was the drawback to a woman's life. According to *adat* or custom law, they were the equals of men. They could be the head of a longhouse, they inherited and owned property on the same basis as men, but they were left with the most tedious work. They did not hunt, they did not fish with nets or harpoons, and until a few years ago they did not go on *bejalai*. On the farm physical strength determined that men cut down trees while women cleared undergrowth, but the prime reason why women

176

did the weeding was because men found it too boring. In everyday matters men had acquired the high ground. They ate first, did no domestic work, and found time to discuss their dreams and their farms while their wives were hard at work.

Nevertheless in one crucial aspect of their lives, women and men did meet as equals. Perhaps it was their failure to be accorded equality elsewhere that explained the Iban women's readiness to mock men on the sensitive subject of their performance in bed. Sowing-time which, given the anthropomorphism of the rice, was redolent with sexuality, offered them the best opportunity. At Nanga Bretik on the Batang Ai, the women strapped huge, mock penises to their waists on the day after the rice was sown, and paraded up and down the gallery making disparaging comparisons between the size of their artificial members and those of the men. The males meanwhile buried their heads in earnest consultation about the prospects for a good harvest, in a vain endeavour not to hear what was being said about them. And whenever a group of women got together at Rumah Langga, the conversation seemed to turn to sex eventually.

It may have been male sensitivity on this score which led to the fashion for the *palang* or penis pin. My ignorance of their function had been dispelled by the unlikely agency of Joseph, the Catholic Iban whom I met at Song while waiting for Tony. He was deeply concerned about the corrupting effect of foreign influences on his people, and one of his examples was the *palang*.

'It was the Chinese who introduced us to the *palang*,' he said disapprovingly. 'No one else would think of such a thing. You know they start by pushing a sliver of bamboo through the penis, and then they gradually enlarge the hole until they can push the pin through. And it is equally bad for the soul because it also provokes wicked thoughts.'

The alleged reward for inserting the little dumb-bells by this excruciating bit of surgery was to make the men irresistible to women. The medical records of army recruits in the 1950s showed that in the district around Kapit almost 40 per cent of the men were fitted with them. Elsewhere the custom was less popular, and fewer than 5 per cent of their other Iban recruits had penis pins. The 1950s were their high point, and since then there has been a steady decline in their use. As a symbol of male over-compensation, however, they continue to exert a strange fascination.

With this exception, sex certainly seemed to figure more largely in women's imaginations than in men's, or at least sexual imagery was much more frequent in their general conversation. The men looked at a wriggling fish and commented on its size, but the women, both on the Bangkit and on the Batang Ai, remarked on the similarity between its movement and someone making love. When I brought back some axe handles from the bazaar, they were immediately criticised by everyone in the longhouse. Mandau and Langga both attempted to explain what was wrong with them, but it was Limau who put the objection most succinctly.

'Those axe handles are no good,' she said scornfully. 'An axe handle should be straight, not curved like an erect penis.'

At fifteen or sixteen, the age when she was ready for wooing, an Iban girl had little excuse for not having a complete understanding of what was involved, and what men expected of her. Not only would she have heard all about it, she would have seen all about it too, for there was no privacy beyond that provided by a mosquito net. What she expected of men was more complex for it involved the very qualities on which upriver society was based.

Traditionally the one outstanding virtue which she looked for was that of *brani* or courage, and a young man who brought back a severed head could expect it to talk for him more seductively than any Romeo. Even Dambak's severe face broke into a smile when she explained the attraction of those grey skulls.

'If a person has taken a head,' she said 'he is brave. A woman favours such a man.' She was just old enought to have been one of the girls whom the *Sarawak Gazette* described as having been transformed into little furies by the sight of a Japanese head.

Yet, even when head-hunting was practised, women tended to favour also men who showed enterprise on *bejalai*. Souvenirs from a successful trading expedition indicated a resourceful, determined character who would make a good husband. It was this that made *bejalai* so crucial to a young man, and one who brought back money he had saved or useful equipment could expect to be well received by a girl. Certainly in one of the best known love songs, head-hunting was referred to simply as a trading expedition;

'Where have you been,' demanded the girl, 'who never touched me at my bed for this whole year? I hope you are dead and become a spirit.'

'I went to another country,' the boy explained, 'and that's why I did not touch you at your bed or sit by your side smelling you.' His journey took him to 'Mukah for rubber-tapping', to 'Bintulu, looking for Segiya jars', and to a dozen other places before he was finally able to take a head and bring it back home to his true love.

There was still the matter of sex appeal. Matu was neither brave nor rich, but that did not stop girls, and respectably married women come to that, shouting and waving at him from the platform when his prau floated into view. He was not particularly handsome, so good looks were evidently less important than vigour, but to judge by the amount of time he spent squinting into a pocket mirror in order to pull individual hairs with a pair of tweezers from his apparently smooth chin, a beard was a handicap. More important than smoothness was cleanliness. Everyone washed at least twice a day, and more often if they had been working outside. The commonest insult was to say that someone smelled. The children would scream at each other, 'You've got a smelly penis', and burst into fits of laughter, and when Jingga got into a drunken quarrel with an old friend, they hung swoonily on to one another's necks slurring 'You smell like pigshit'. 'You smell like pigshit too'. The first step for any youth hoping for success was into the river with a bar of soap in his hand and a clean sarong waiting on the beach.

Almost inevitably my love affair with all things Iban soon crystallised into an urge to find an Iban girl to *ngayap* or woo. Unfortunately there were no unmarried women in Rumah Langga. The nearest lived two hours upstream in Membuas's longhouse. The offer of a further bout in our drinking contest provided an excuse for me to visit, but with Tony in his driving mood there was no time for self-indulgence.

In retrospect, the atmosphere of the festival had offered the clearest opportunities. The young men had returned from *bejalai*, bringing with them an atmosphere of excitement and possibility. The girls were expected to persuade male guests to drink their share, and more, of the *tuak*, while the men were supposed to put on a show of resistance. There was, therefore, much scope for body contact as glasses were thrust forward and pushed away. *Tuak* once offered had to be drunk, but a man could refuse unless the girl drank with him or, as a last resort, until she had sung him a praise-song. In the intricate allusions and plain nonsense of its words, quick-witted girls often hid private messages which only a lover could decipher. Who else (other than Freud) would have understood her when she sang of the delights awaiting a 'smooth stone squeezed between roots' when it found an expectant 'underground hole wrapped in grass'?

Dancing presented a more straightforward opportunity for close encounters. Late in the evening, after everyone had eaten and the men had had a chance to talk, the women, usually prompted by Pantai and her friend Min, brought out the gongs and drums. At Rumah Langga the instruments consisted of a rack of five gongs, arranged on a frame and played like a xylophone, two long cylindrical drums beaten with the palms and fingers, and a large hanging gong struck with a piece of wood. Only the women played, usually under Mangan's direction, and though she yelled fiercely when things went wrong, the performances were ragged. This was unfortunate because at other longhouses where both men and women made up the bands, the best music was as intricate in its rhythms and runs as Balinese gamelan. First Pantai and Min would perform, the former conscientiously following the steps, the latter with the graceful languor of someone twice her age. Then they turned on the men and with muscles hardened by hours of pounding rice, ruthlessly frog-marched them on to the floor.

Jingga was the only male to mount an effective riposte. His dance became an elegant mime of a girl hunting for her sarong. Once it had been found and put on, she took a bucket and some clothes down to the river. There she scrubbed her clothes, all the while darting covert glances over her shoulder. Keeping time to the music, Jingga mimed her relief on seeing the coast was clear, and tiptoed over to an imaginary rock. Slowly it dawned on the audience that this was the tale of a young girl, and no one doubted that it was either Pantai or Min. Then it became clear that she was looking for a place to defecate unobserved, and the accompaniment grew hopelessly erratic as the women at the gongs doubled up with laughter. Jingga squatted nervously, his face darted from side to side like a startled deer, his eyes screwed up with effort, then opened wide in relief. Hurriedly he wiped his bottom with a stick, and picking up the bucket nonchalantly strolled away. It was a virtuoso performance.

When the dancing was over and the instruments put away, the women and married men retired to the apartments, while the bachelors and visitors laid themselves down on sleeping mats in the gallery. Then, in a longhouse where there were unmarried women, it was not so much the frenzied scratching of the dogs that kept you awake as the furtive movements of young men on the prowl. When the unmarried women in Langga's longhouse left after the festival, the young men, with Matu in the lead, soon took to disappearing on night-time visits to other longhouses on the river.

The rhythms of purposeful, food-producing activity which everyone else followed did not seem to apply to Matu. All his energies were devoted to hunting game and women, and sleeping off the consequences.

'What do you do when you go wooing?' I asked.

Before he had a chance to reply, his mother, Limau, chipped

in with the obvious answer, 'You throw the girl's sarong over her head.'

Matu took this as something of a reflection on his expertise. 'No, no,' he said seriously. 'You must talk to her first. The talk is very important.'

'What do you say to her?' I asked.

It was Bulik's turn to interrupt. 'You say, I'll give you thirty dollars if you'll sleep with me,' he suggested with an evil grin.

Matu sulked at this and refused to divulge any more of his secret. In the vacuum, someone else chipped in with the observation that it depended on the woman. 'You screw the bad women,' he said, 'but you woo the good women.'

Everyone agreed, but this variant on the masculine double standard was not much help. In the past there had been a general belief in the moral laxity of the Iban, the nineteenth-century missionaries being particularly quick to picture them as depraved and licentious. It was difficult to know whether to believe the accusations of men who resisted the temptation of those smooth brown bodies, or the defence of Charles Brooke who succumbed repeatedly.

'Strangers generally look on their conduct . . . as being remarkably volatile and disreputable,' he wrote; 'and this idea has been circulated by the teachers of the Gospel. But an impartial observer, after making inquiry, will find there are many more penalties attached to their peccadilloes than, I believe, are found under similar circumstances in Europe.'

It was Ayum who explained the chief rule which, however unfairly, applied to the girl. If she were to become pregnant, she had to be able to name the father. *Adat* required this to be done within three months, on the common-sense grounds that after that time desperation might persuade a pregnant woman to name anyone. If the named man refused to marry her, he had to pay a heavy fine which was split three ways, between the woman, the longhouse where she lived, and the unborn child. Should no one accept paternity, a pig had to be sacrificed to compensate for the misdeed, but that did not remove the shame of a fatherless baby. Faced with that possibility, most women preferred to have an abortion, and *adat* prescribed no penalty in that case, provided she was unmarried.

It was, therefore, imperative for a girl to know who her lover was and where he came from, so that if necessary he could be forced to acknowledge his responsibility. Naturally enough, the further off he lived the more likely he was to be rebuffed, and for a visitor the need for a persuasive tongue became the more important. At one of the longhouses we visited, Ayum went to *ngayap* a girl who had given him some *tuak*, and faced the triple objection that he was a stranger, he was visiting for one night only, and he lived a long distance away. His response provided a nice example of Iban eloquence.

'When a man comes to a strange longhouse from far away,' he said, 'what can he do if he sees an attractive girl? He is like a traveller who is caught in a sudden rainstorm. He must find shelter immediately, where he is. It is raining now and you are my shelter.' Then he added, honestly perhaps but less than tactfully, 'Of course when the rain stops, the traveller moves on.' She was not won over.

A man had fewer concerns in wooing. Theoretically a notorious philanderer should have faced the objection that he would not make a good husband, but Matu apparently faced no such obstacle. Although he was only twenty-five years old, he had by his own estimate been married six times, and still there were shadows under his eyes whenever he returned from one of his expeditions. His secret, as he explained when I knew him better, was that he restricted his activities entirely to married women, because they appreciated him more, 'but', he added 'never if the man's around the longhouse, however old he is and however young the woman – it's not worth the risk.'

The risk arose from the punishment which the cuckolded husband was entitled to inflict. 'Should a husband suspect a man of having committed adultery with his wife,' wrote a nineteenth-century observer, 'he says nothing about it, but prepares a club and in company with a friend or two lurks about watching for

183

the offender; he may meet him going to or returning from bathing, and wherever he does meet him he is entitled to strike him, only he must not go into the man's house for the purpose.'

Convention demanded that only a club should be used in order to reduce the chance of murder, but since the weapon was carved from *bilian* or ironwood, and was armed with sharp spikes, the injuries inflicted could be horrific. The *Sarawak Gazette* carried a report that a man called Sureng, 'had been violently assaulted with a *bilian* club by Saweng, and that there was no chance of the former living. Sureng had his head broken open, collar bones and left arm fractured, and right leg fractured near the knee.'

Adat, ever anxious to preserve the peace, proscribed any retaliation of this kind once the deceived husband had publicly accused his deceiver, by killing a fowl and hurling it at him. Thus publicly accused, the adulterer was tried and if found guilty was liable to the same penalty as that imposed for wounding someone accidentally – a heavy fine and the sacrifice of a pig and a fowl. It was enough simply to flirt with a man's wife for him to exact a fine, which was what happened during the festival when Langga's nephew felt that the seventeen-year-old Alo was paying too much attention to his wife. A hurried meeting was called in Langga's apartment, where Alo was found guilty of stirring up ill-feeling and fined.

This served to convince me that adultery was wrong, and banishing all thoughts of the exquisite Sebang from my mind, I decided to wait until the opportunity arose to go to Membuas's longhouse. When it came at last, the consequences led me to believe that there must have been a bad dream which I had failed to remember, or at least an unlucky bird whose call my dullness did not heed.

Michael had by then returned from Kuching, to find Jingga adopting a reproachful, distant manner towards him. He lost few opportunities of referring to the kindnesses he had done us, but he did so without the old endearments of 'friend' or 'son'. Now he called Michael *tuan*, or lord, and his voice had the tone of one who has loved not wisely but too well. Michael's temper was

184

rubbed raw within minutes. He decided to escape upriver with Ayum, and his mood did not improve when I insisted on coming too.

Membuas, however, was delighted to see me, and lost no time in bringing out *tuak* for the return match. The acidity of that brew would have burnt lines in an etcher's plate. Membuas seemed unaffected, and if his pose was a bluff, it succeeded. When he pushed the third pint across, I tapped the bowl apologetically and conceded victory to him. Even so, I was too late; that night burning stomach pains evaporated any thought of love.

The next day we went fishing higher up, where the hills flattened out into rolling country and the river flowed at a more leisurely pace. Up here much of the jungle was still untouched, and trees of huge girth crowded the river bank. On the hills there were farms, rubber plantations and pepper gardens. It was the sort of country that traditionally minded Iban dreamed of.

Membuas must have been a good augurer, and it bothered me that I could detect no particular sensitivity or insight in him. If Mandau resembled an accountant, Membuas was a senior company executive, a solid, reliable heavyweight. Yet the fact that the longhouse had made good use of its resources and avoided disastrous feuds was undeniable evidence of his skill.

Eventually I decided that it was no coincidence that Mandau and he had such prosaic personalities. In a divided world, spirituality or other-worldliness might be needed to divine the will of the gods, but here it required a practical, clear-headed appraisal of all the information available from the omens. It was a job closer to a company manager's than a priest's. The effectiveness of his skill was apparent wherever we looked, but its limitations only emerged that evening.

Most of the families were still out gathering fruit when we returned, but they began to drift back while we sat talking with Membuas's wife. He himself had just come in when there was a commotion from the beach. Men began running up the ladder shouting wildly for the women, for help, for cushions, for water. At once some of the women began to scream, some rushed to

185

the platform and shrieked for their husbands, others ran to and fro between the platform and their apartments. The screams grew louder as a man climbed heavily up the ladder with another man tied to his back. The path from the boats, up the ladder and along the platform was marked with dark drops of blood.

Membuas's wife began to shout orders. Her voice was high and strained but under control. A mattress and cushions were brought into the gallery, and a sack was laid on them to protect them from the blood. A dozen men relieved the bearer and laid the man on the mattress. His face was pale and beaded with sweat. Round his left thigh was tied a rag bandage sodden with blood, and when it was removed the cause of the screams was revealed. His thigh was split open from side to side by a deep wound which had severed the muscle so that the ends were hanging out. Remorselessly the blood kept seeping up, and however often it was swabbed away its red sheen soon re-covered the wound.

The man's name was Langgai. He had been cutting branches high up in a fruit tree when his bush-knife slipped from his hand. Unable to move away, he had tried to kick it aside but had misjudged its fall. That had happened two hours earlier, far upriver, and now with evening coming on it was too late to get him down to the clinic even if he could have survived the loss of blood during the journey. Already his feet were icy cold and his eyes kept turning up into his head.

The shouting had died away. Instead a dense and largely silent crowd had formed around his bed. To keep him conscious was their prime concern, for once his soul had wandered from his body it might never return. They had propped him up with cushions, and his wife was feeding him raw sugar cane, but beyond that there was no more that they could do, other than call upon the spirits.

Already the plates of rice and eggs were being brought out, and Membuas's wife insisted that a white spirit make the offering. Michael refused point-blank, and at that moment the dream of a unitary world, of placating the spirits and reading the auguries,

186

began to slip towards nightmare. Every time that Langgai slid
into unconsciousness his relations screamed to prevent his soul
leaving him. The blind panic in their voices plucked at my
concentration as I tried to build the familiar pile of sticky rice,
eggs and tobacco leaf. Behind me Langgai was quite possibly
dying, and the plate in front of me was all that could be done to
keep him alive.

When the pile was complete, I began with the customary
'Howa, Howa, Howa', and then stopped. The only prayer I knew
was the one calling for more rice, more money, more everything,
and since that was hardly appropriate, I continued in English. I
recollect the words with embarrassment:

'If there is anyone out there listening, gods of the forest, gods
of the rice, Pulang Gana, Singalang Burong, anyone, you must
come at once to save Langgai, to stop the bleeding. Come and
save Langgai.'

Even as I spoke I realised that this was absurd. It was panic,
an abnegation not only of my own intelligence, but of the culture
in which I was brought up. But a life was in the balance, and
superstition required you to perform its rituals however absurd.

It was Michael who saved his life. Prepared for any emergency,
it seemed, he had packed an elastic bandage into a small medical
kit. A tourniquet round the man's upper thigh slowed the bleeding while a prau was sent to fetch our larger medical bag from
Rumah Langga. It took two hours to return, but by then the
blood was beginning to clot. As best we could, we stuffed bits of
severed muscle back inside the wound, and tugged the flaps of
skin together. With plastic sutures to close the wound, crepe
bandage to bind it, and painkillers to comfort the victim, the
achievements of Western technology had never been more palpable. His breathing soon became easier, and before long warmth
began to return to his feet. He was still weak, but his mind had
regained alertness, and it looked as though he would recover.
According to Membuas that was the outcome that might have
been expected.

Before Langgai had set out for work, his wife had told him

that she had had a bad dream. What it was she could not remember, just that it was bad and that he must not go out. A little impatiently he agreed to stay at home, but at lunchtime he decided that he could not afford to waste any more time. Picking up his bush-knife, he left the longhouse to get fruit. Without exception, everyone who heard the story agreed that what saved his life was the decision to stay at home for the morning. Had he gone to work straightaway, he would certainly have died. It was an object lesson that one should never ignore a bad dream.

The relief at his escape from the shadowy land of Sabayan coupled with the presence of strange males in the longhouse was excuse enough for a party, and after we had eaten the gongs were brought out and the women began to dance. Unlike the women at Langga's house, they were large and solidly built. It may have been the feeding because Membuas was far beefier than his brother Langga, but there was also more virgin forest here and perhaps the task of cutting it down developed larger muscles. Whatever the reason, my feet did not even drag on the floor but kicked unavailingly in the air when the girls turned to fetch out men to dance for them.

One of the superb caryatids who carried me on to the floor wore a red blouse, and when I finished my Highland Fling she smiled then lowered her head. Someone had a tape-cassette, and I persuaded the girl in the red blouse to try a Western dance. The novelty of being held made her rigid with fright, and her magnificent body felt as though it were carved of wood. Nevertheless, I felt that this first contact could lead on to more.

As usual the furtive rustlings began soon after the longhouse had retired to sleep, but instead of trying to sleep I decided to join the rustlers. Almost at once I bumped into Matu, who had come up to *ngayap* independently, and persuaded him to help my attempt at wooing. He looked a little doubtful, and before agreeing repeated his remark about the importance of talk.

The girl in the red blouse was called Se, and Matu led me to her apartment. The door was locked, but with the noiseless skill of the practised wooer, he put a ladder against the wall, and climbed up into the loft. I could just hear the faintest bump as he let himself down inside, then the bolt was drawn back and the door gently pulled open. The casual conversation at Rumah Langga had created the impression in my mind that wooing was too open a business to attract any attention, but Matu's elaborate precautions against making the slightest noise alarmed me. Suddenly the whole business seemed fraught with hazard. I was after all breaking into the home of a stranger whose daughter I was proposing to seduce, whose language I could scarcely speak, and who to judge by Matu's precautions was at least extremely dangerous and at the most might be a head hunter. What if he woke up? Would he be able to tell in the dark that I was a mere seducer and not a would-be adulterer who deserved to be beaten to pulp with a spiked club? In any case, what did Iban fathers do to mere seducers? I turned to ask Matu, but he, having done his part, had stolen away, leaving me to find out for myself.

The room was lit by an oil lamp in the middle of the floor. By its yellow flame I could see two mosquito nets, one spread out above a four-poster bed in the corner, the other strung out over a mattress on the floor nearby. It was impossible to see through the netting, and the thought of lifting the wrong one and coming face to face with an irate father made my blood run cold. Then I started to think rationally. It was obvious that the parents would sleep in the four-poster. I crept quietly to the mattress, and had my hand on the mosquito net when from beneath it came a long, burbling and distinctly male snore. I stepped hastily back, and to my horror landed on a creaking board. In utter silence I stood stock still, but the snoring never ceased. Reassured, I tiptoed towards the bed in the corner, cautiously lifted the net, then dropped it immediately. There were two bodies sleeping there. I raced back to the gallery and found Matu stalking another apartment.

'Two in the bed,' I whispered.

He looked puzzled. I mimed the situation, but before I had finished he had gone to investigate. Left to myself I looked up and down the darkened gallery. It was like a burglars' convention, the place was alive with men stealing guiltily from door to door. One of them turned out to be Ayum, and not trusting to my scanty supply of Iban, I asked him if he would stand by to translate in an emergency. It has to be said for Ayum that he gave everything when he laughed, especially when it was silent, and it was ages before he could draw sufficient breath to agree. When Matu returned, he had a grin on his face. One of the bodies was a bolster, he claimed. Convinced he was wrong, and certain that my Iban would not cope with wooing two girls at once, I insisted that Ayum keep his word and come with me on my second visit.

This time it was reassuring to hear that deliberate, regular snore from the mattress, and I lost no time in making for the bed. To my relief Matu was right, it was a bolster beside the girl. I moved it away and sat down beside her. She was wearing a sarong, but since it was wrapped tightly around her muscular legs, I could see no way of following Limau's advice about throwing it over her head. Her face was hidden in shadow, and she seemed to be sleeping heavily. She must know, I thought, that some young man would come to her bed, and after all there had been those glances we had exchanged while dancing. I laid my hand on her thigh. Her regular breathing continued undisturbed. It struck me that her sleep might be a pretence. I moved my hand to her hip. Still she lay without moving. I tried to marshal my stock of Iban words into a loving phrase to whisper in her ear, but my vocabulary had disappeared. It would have to be the language of touch then. I leaned over the recumbent body, and suddenly she came to life. She sat up, her superb shoulders and breasts heaving, and let out a volley of astonished Iban of which I could not understand a word.

'It's all right,' I whispered feebly in English.

More Iban, and it seemed tinged with outrage. Talk, I began to see, was important. Not a single word came to mind, so I patted her reassuringly instead. She pushed my hand away indignantly. When she spoke again the outrage was more marked, and my soothing words in English could not stem the

190

flow. It seemed impossible that her father should continue to snore undisturbed through the tirade.

'Say it more quietly,' I whispered, and put my finger to my lips, 'Shush'.

In the momentary silence which this produced, I heard a smothered chuckle from the end of the bed, and against the flame of the lamp, I saw a crouched figure stealing towards the door. With a surge of relief I recognised the silhouette.

'Ayum,' I cried desperately, 'Ayum, come and explain.'

If Se had been outraged before, it was nothing to her fury when a second man came and sat on her bed. My admiration for Ayum's eloquence grew amazingly as her protests died away, and she sat back glancing from him to me. Then she asked where I came from, where I was living, and where I would be going to after I left the longhouse. I countered with a compliment on the grace of her dancing. She said she was tired and had to work on the farm in the morning. I replied that she was very beautiful. Given the handicap of wooing through an interpreter who had difficulty in keeping a straight face, I felt that we were making ground. She pointed out that she did not know who I was. I thought of saying I was a white *antu*, then decided this might frighten her, and was floundering for a deft reply when I noticed Ayum's lip twitching. It was contagious. I turned away, but could not hold back the hysteria that infected me. I fought to beat it down, but each snore from the next-door bed brought it back. Se's face took on a dangerous frown, then she too succumbed to the fever. Huddled under the mosquito net, the three of us giggled to the point of choking, and like children every effort to control ourselves produced a fresh outburst.

Suddenly the snores from her father's bed ceased. I sobered instantly and punched Ayum into silence. Pictures of *bilian* clubs flashed unnervingly into my mind, I saw the head-hunters' swords which the warriors wielded in the *gawai kenyalang*, and I recalled vividly the skulls hanging in their nets. It was a time for cowardice, not gallantry. I fled, and was followed soon

191

afterwards by Ayum scarcely able to walk from the effort to suppress his laughter.

There could be no possibility of keeping such an encounter secret in a longhouse, but even so I was surprised how quickly the news travelled, for when we returned the next morning to Rumah Langga, there was a circle of advisers waiting to tell me what I should have done. Dambak repeated the impractical advice about throwing the girl's skirt over her face, but the general opinion was that Se's questions needed more reassuring answers than they had received. I should have said who I was and where I came from. What no one could understand was my fear of her father's wrath. Why should that have concerned me? A father, it seemed, would never interfere with a nocturnal visitor to his daughter's bedside, unless he appeared several nights in succession. At that point he would feel obliged to ask the visitor when the wedding would take place. Sex simply was not an important enough matter to be worth heating up the longhouse and disturbing the spirits.

However humiliating it was to think of my nerve buckling at a mere cessation of snoring, I could claim that in the Western scale of values, sex was what bore the psychological burden, and it was not an activity which could take place easily under the parental gaze. For the Iban it was death, heavy with auguries, omens and offerings, that carried the psychological weight. In a single evening the contrast in attitudes to the twin poles of human existence had been starkly presented, and Langgai's near fatal accident had brought home forcibly the advantage of Western values. It also dealt a mortal blow to my passion for the Iban way. In the choice between modern and traditional, divided and unitary, the balance had swung the other way. Put crudely, I felt that the availability of painkillers was worth more than a night of love.

12

Cosmic Errors

As THOUGH THE natural cycle of the expedition had passed its apogee, the end began to come into sight for one project after another. The day in the life had been ticked off twice, as well as the life of the dog, the hunt, longhouse interiors, longhouse exteriors, forest with figures, and river with figures. There had been dumb shots, dead shots, cover shots and context shots – whatever they were. Lines had been put through anxious little queries in my notebook – how big are the farms? ask Mandau about bad birds; what *does* Matu say to them?

Tony was now planning to leave for Kuching, to send off another fifty rolls of film before they were damaged by the heat. Then would come a brief return to the Batang Ai to record the burning of the forest at Nanga Bretik, and his task would be complete. Serious academic work was looming for both Michael and James, and they too were beginning to look beyond the end of the expedition. For my part, I was racking my brains to think what crucially obvious subject I had failed to cover. Shortly before we left I realised that I had failed to ask anyone at Rumah Langga about head-hunting.

There were no tattooed hands, but I wanted to know what they would do if presented with the chance to take a head. Langga was the obvious person to ask, given his capacity for concentrated emotion. The occasion arose at one of the gossip evenings on the gallery.

They were talking of going on *bejalai* and Ayum mentioned an occasion when a Chinese confidence trickster tried to fool him into buying a false permit. Langga gave a harsh laugh. He too had encountered the wily Chinese, this time offering a discount for a group of Iban flying from Kuching to Sibu. 'I told the man, I have never heard of anyone getting a discount on this flight before,' he declared. 'You are just trying to trick these people. You clear off, and if I ever find you trying to trick Iban again, I'll cut your head off. They cleared off fast.'

Two boys, Bagang, and the would-be seducer, Alo, both listened wide-eyed to these stories, and soon others joined the group, Tigang, Jingga and Nyanggau among them. The talk turned to the confrontation with Indonesia during the 1960s. James remarked that his brother-in-law had once found himself alone in charge of an Indonesian prisoner. 'Why didn't he chop off his head?' Langga demanded fiercely. 'All's fair in war. If I had been guarding him, I'd have chopped off his head.'

The aggression that burned in his eyes when he spoke like that was convincing enough, but I wondered whether he was inclined to be vainglorious. The answer came with the story of the longhouse's incursion into the war. It occurrred in 1965 when news that an Indonesian column was coming down into the Bangkit inspired Langga and some two hundred other men from the river to try their hand. Just as they were setting off they heard a bad bird, and the more experienced members of the party insisted on turning back. But not the young men. ' "Stuff that" we said,' Langga recalled. ' "You only live once – we're going on." ' (This was James's racy translation.) And so they did, canoeing straight into an Indonesian ambush.

Langga described the confusion in his usual declamatory style. How the three men in the leading boat were captured. How the rest had jumped out of their boats and hidden under the banks of the river. How Tigang had stood stock still in the middle of the river while the bullets pinged off the water. And how he had refused to move even when they shouted at him.

'I stood there because they were firing from so far off,' Tigang explained. 'I didn't think shot-guns would reach so far – I didn't know about the range of a rifle then.'

Langga had yelled at Nyanggau, who was Tigang's nephew, to pull him down.

'Not me,' Nyanggau snapped back. 'Let the old fool be, I'm not getting him.'

Finally Langga rushed out and hauled him under the shelter of the bank. The circle of bronzed bodies pressed closer in the glow of the oil lamp, gripped by the drama of the confrontation.

'And then what did you do?' someone asked excitedly from the audience.

'What did we do?' Langga demanded in ringing tones. 'We ran away as fast as we possibly could.'

He was, I decided, a pragmatist, not a boaster, and a pragmatist probably would take a head if the opportunity arose.

Persistent rumours continued to crop up of surreptitious head taking. In the late 1970s, some 6,000 Koreans, employed in the construction of a liquid gas terminal at Bintulu, had to be housed in a special compound after bar-room brawls with Iban workers led to fifteen of them being killed and losing their heads. Period-ically the *Sarawak Gazette* carried reports of murders which also mentioned that the victim had been decapitated. It was tempting to take such cases as justification for continuing to label the Iban, 'The head-hunters of Sarawak'. The conviction was growing in me, nevertheless, that the old title was not only out of date but positively misleading.

When Dambak spoke of the courage in taking heads, it could hardly have been in relation to their acquisition. Any head would do – man, woman or child – and the low-browed skull hanging outside Langga's apartment which his father had lopped off had once been covered in tawny fur and belonged to an orang-utan. The real courage lay in the head-hunter's ability to confront the living dead. If Saul's shade was frightening, how much more terrifying would be the spirit of a young person whose body had been ferociously attacked and denied burial? To take and tame such a force was the ultimate challenge.

195

Yet heads were never more than a means to an end. Their seed promoted a good harvest, and abundant rice earned jars and gongs which alone counted as the symbols of a successful life. An enterprising trader could achieve the same goal by bringing back a chain-saw or an outboard engine. It might be difficult to see how trade could bring the awful glory that came from possessing a dead person's head, but Langga himself admitted that what had once been a sign of highest courage was now out of date.

'Nowadays we don't look for bravery,' he said in a calmer voice. 'What is important is the reputation that comes from good farming or success in *bejalai*.'

The relish with which he had described the challenge of *bejalai*, the deceitfulness of shopkeepers, or the miserliness of employers, suggested that the trophies brought back from the city were as hard won as any head. They might not bear seed but they could help towards a better harvest, and their spirits were powerful. When a relative of Engkin's brought back a new chain-saw during the festival, an offering of rice and eggs was made to it. Then both chain-saw and rice were placed by the apartment wall and wrapped in a ceremonial blanket for forty-eight hours while the spirit dined off the soul-food before it.

When Jingga's *kenyalang* flew off to confront hostile elements far away rather than Kayans or Ukit or people close at hand, it reflected the change that had taken place. The possibility of inflicting sudden death was too remote, instead the great test against which a man had to measure his nerve and courage was the outside world. The resemblance was perhaps closer than the Iban imagined, for like death the power of the outside world could be robbed and used, but only at the risk of being overwhelmed by it.

Yet their history showed an astonishing capacity to absorb alien influences: from the Bukitan they had picked up jungle skills; from the Kayan tattooing and dancing; from the Malays, piracy; from the British, litigation, guns, trousers and rubber trees; from the Chinese, penis pins; from the Japanese, outboard

196

motors; from the Germans, chain-saws; and from the Americans, T-shirts. Whether this flexibility could cope with the future was more doubtful. It would rest largely with the two boys, Bagang and Alo, who had to face the more insidious challenge of education, religion, and cash.

Like the vast majority of upriver Iban, Bagang had left school at twelve, after four years in the little white building at the mouth of the Bangkit. At fourteen, he could write his name, and speak some Bahasa, the official Malaysian language, but most of his education had taken place in the longhouse. From his father he had learned how to carve the stock of a harpoon and to hammer nails into barbs, and when he went fishing he picked up from Bulik the technique of watching for the flash of a fish's belly as it turned to give him his target. On the farm, he assimilated woodcraft while felling trees for the rice, and discovered how different strains of rice fared in various conditions while he guarded the growing crop.

Above all he was learning respect for experience. Nothing he did had not been done before. His elders had already perfected the skills he was beginning to practise, and he could only profit from their advice.

Alo, on the other hand, belonged to the tiny minority who had gone on to secondary education, and now he was waiting to go to sixth form college. He was highly intelligent, and his habit of thought had become challenging rather than accepting; he wanted to know why things were done in a particular way, not how. His fine for flirting might have been anticipated, since he was Matu's nephew, but not his resentment of it. If he stayed in the longhouse, his intelligence would be invaluable for the changes that were bound to come, but the amorphous authority of *adat* could not easily find a place for an independent line of conduct.

Religion presented a different kind of challenge to the existing order. One upriver Iban put his finger on the way a unitary view of the world imposed conformity when he explained to a missionary why he could not become a Christian:

197

'We don't worship unless it has something to do with our work,' he said. 'We don't work unless it has something to do with our worship ... I have not become a Christian, because I cannot. I need help on my farm for planting, weeding, harvesting, and to get help I must give it in return. I can only get it and give it if I farm with the others and observe the same periods of work and rest as they do.'

Sometimes Christianity was grafted on to the Iban's existing beliefs, on the pragmatic grounds that it had proved its power by helping to make the Europeans powerful. Thus, after *manggol* rituals on the farm, a man might also say a Christian prayer, or a pig might be sacrificed on a Saint's Day. But otherwise, either a convert left the longhouse, or the community became Christian.

Muslim influence, if it had any effect at all, was more drastic. The first stumbling block to conversion was the prohibition on pork, which ruled out the Iban's greatest delicacy. But the other obstacle was more profound. An Iban might become a Christian and remain an Iban, but if he became a Muslim he was then by definition a Malay. Conversion could be advantageous to an educated Iban in government service, but it was impossible in the longhouse.

The most dangerous aspect of the outside world was cash. Essentially the longhouse was run as a food economy. A person might fish rather than hunt, weed rather than hew, weave baskets instead of cleaning grit from the rice, but each job had to be done if bellies were to be filled. The yardstick by which the value of work was measured was the effort required and the attention paid to the spirits.

Although the apartments were filled with goods which had been bought for cash on *bejalai*, money played little part in daily life. In a good year a family would sell rice, pepper and fruit in the bazaar in Song, and buy petrol, salt, sugar and cloth. In a bad year they might have to buy rice if their neighbours had none to spare, and in an emergency they would have to sell a gong or a blanket to pay for it.

All this was made possible by the despised Chinese shopkeepers who acted as bankers extending credit where necessary, as middle men for the goods the Iban wished to sell, and as hoteliers if they needed to stay overnight. Since all transactions could be carried out in one place, cash exchanges were kept to a minimum even here. Although the Iban complained constantly of being cheated by the Chinese, they were reluctant to patronise the few establishments run by their own people, because the latter were not as keen to extend credit as the Chinese for whom it represented a major source of profit.

By catering for all their needs, the shopkeepers effectively insulated them from the outside world, and allowed them to return unscathed to their life upriver. There the mediums of exchange were rice and labour. Money was for use in the outside world. Among themselves the only time it was needed was to pay Langga to have their rice mechanically husked in his petrol-driven mill. Although he only charged $2.80 a hundredweight, it was a perpetual source of resentment.

The alternative was suggested by a longhouse half an hour from Song. It was a permanent building set on concrete foundations, and run on a cash basis. Many of the men worked on construction sites in Song, and spent their spare time raising cash crops like rubber and pepper. Their earnings were spent in the longhouse shop run by the headman. A diesel-driven generator provided electricity for lighting and television at a cost of several dollars a day per family.

The effect was to splinter the cohesion which marked the traditional longhouse. The difference between the richest and poorest was emphasised by clothes and equipment, and the women and the old took a clearly subservient place to active men because their work did not earn money.

Paradoxically a *gawai kenyalang* celebrated there was not only more elaborate than Jingga's, but far more correct in its adherence to traditional detail. Their bards chanted the longest sacred songs, and the warriors clad in fur surcoats slashed at the skulls with genuine fervour. All the same I wouldn't have traded Jingga's festival for theirs. Now that I knew Time-Life were going

199

to show the upriver Iban as they really were, I found Jingga's slightly threadbare display quite endearing. There was besides that a curious symmetry between our fortunes and his. We had each of us rescued the other's project. He too after an uncertain start could now congratulate himself on having carried out all that he set out to do. It was time for the travellers to return home, and as our departure became imminent, he arranged to bring his *kenyalang* back from its long journey to distant countries.

The hornbill effigy had continued to look down on the long-house while the guests departed, while Saul's body was borne away to the graveyard, and while the hunters returned for the feast to mark the end of mourning. All that time its spirit had roamed land and sea, but now it was coming home.

A crowd assembled on the platform while Engkin shinned up the pole to remove the bird. It was a long job, and the band which was playing grew tired of banging gongs and began to fade away until Mangan galvanised them into activity again.

'They have no sense of timing,' Limau remarked disgustedly.

'None,' said Langga. 'It sounds like a crowd of people farting.'

At last the painted effigy was brought down and placed in Jingga's arms. He received it like a long-lost lover. And so the festival drew towards an end in the same endearing fashion in which it had been conducted. And the pleasure on Jingga's face made up for any shortcomings. For him it was clear that the band played in tune, that the effigy was a masterpiece, and that the perfection of this moment reflected a similar perfection in his fortunes. Beaming with affection, he toured the longhouse followed by a chorus of four men who repeated his chant:

'The hornbill is coming back. It is walking along the platform. I am coming back to my home.'

Up the gallery he came, swinging the bird from side to side, ducking its beak up and down, lost in his happiness.

'I have come back from the sea. Back from the Caves of Wind and the Hall of Thunder. Back to the place I know.'

In front of every apartment an offering was laid out, and after each offering had been made *tuak* was offered to the effigy, to Jingga, to the chorus, and to everyone present. Progress was slow. Soon their voices grew hoarse and Jingga was stumbling over the words.

'Listen to that,' Nyanggau groaned. 'Pigs sing sweeter.'

No one paid attention any longer. Eighteen-month-old Suda was hogging the limelight for the women, and the men were watching Langga trying to repair a chain-saw. Its roar drowned out the invocation of the tenth offering and tenth sacrificial fowl. Two more to go, and the rice wine was having its usual effect.

'It's a farting drink,' Limau observed confidentially as Jingga wobbled off to apartment eleven. 'Your belly swells up then – fooo – it goes down a bit – fooo – a bit more – fooo – fooo – the whole night until your belly is quite small again.'

When the last family had been visited, the bird was taken up to the loft above Jingga's apartment, and with tears in his eyes he made his own offering of rice and eggs in the dark, cramped space between mats and rice bins. Tenderly he wrapped the effigy and offering in a ceremonial blanket and placed it in its nest. The bird was home, the wealth it had found would surely be waiting for him.

I hoped it was. He would enjoy wealth, and as the most emotionally expressive man in Rumah Langga his enjoyment would be shared. More selfishly, it was difficult not to feel that our lives had been so deeply dependent on each other that his success would guarantee ours, and vice versa.

The prognostications were mixed. Weeks of dry weather had almost guaranteed a good burn, but they had been followed by ferocious thunderstorms darkening the day to such an extent that lamps were lit to provide beacons to the souls of men absent on *bejalai*. In the division of our goods before we left, Jingga had received our Tilley lamps and fishing-nets, but the real prize had as usual gone to Langga who had claimed, in his most predatory voice, the axe. Jingga responded by waking Michael at 5.30 on the day we left to broach for the final time the prospect of his taking an Iban wife. He was no more successful than before, but as a result the packing of the prau took place in our customary jagged temper.

When it came to saying goodbye, however, all other feelings were washed away by misery. The affection I felt had deepened so gradually that until then I had hardly been aware of it. From being a community to be studied, they had become intimates from whom it was painful to depart. Several men including Matu and Bulik, who were going on *bejalai*, decided to come with us, and the doleful partings spread gloom everywhere.

For Bulik the farewell was particularly painful because his wife, Orin, who had always accompanied him on *bejalai* before, was staying behind on this occasion. She would be in the care of Jingga and Dambak during his absence, but that made it no easier. However faithful, she would have to live alone for the eleven months of the year during which he was working. She might well suspect that he would contract a semi-permanent marriage with a woman at the camp, as often happened, and she would find that male visitors to the longhouse were, like Matu, not particularly scrupulous about the sanctity of marriage. The model for most men, married or not, was provided by none other than Singalang Burong. According to the best known of the epics sung at a *gawai kenyalang*, when he and his companions arrive at the longhouse for the festival they pause before going in, and Singalang Burong warns them to get their excuses ready for when they go back home:

> 'So, if some of us get finger marks and scratches on our backs
> and ribs,
> On our return, do not show them to wives and sweethearts,
> If found, say they were made when playing with the children.'

The strain of these suspicions broke through as an offering was being made for Bulik's safety and success. While the family were still sitting round the half-empty plates and the basket piled with rice and eggs, he suddenly made an impassioned speech.

Here he was on the point of departure, he exclaimed, and how was he to know that his wife would be faithful in his absence?

His eyes were red with tears, and his normally round and smiling face was a mask of misery. Mandau replied angrily that as Orin's father he would personally guarantee that she would remain faithful.

'If any man tries to seduce her,' he cried out, 'I will beat him unconscious with a club.'

Mangan too was incensed at the imputation cast at her daughter. She was a good girl, she said, and a hard worker, and there was no justification for levelling such a charge. 'If she fondles anyone in your absence,' she said, 'it will be your child, and no one else.' Then, like the loving mother she was, she added, 'She is my daughter and always will be – whatever happens.'

Throughout these tirades, Bulik clutched his child, the obnoxious Nyandang, in his arms, and let the tears stream unhindered down his cheeks. Unconscious of his role in the drama, the little boy gazed abstractedly over his father's elbow and occasionally picked his nose. Orin herself sat silently, gazing at her delicate ankles, until at last, without having said a word, she brought the scene to an end by getting to her feet and shutting herself in the apartment.

Her refusal to defend herself might well have sprung from the wish to avoid an argument with her husband on the point of his departure. Most of the wives in the longhouse seemed to show no such restraint, and Ayum put a very different construction on her behaviour. *Adat* prescribed stiff penalties for wrongful accusations, and it was immaterial that they were made in the heat of a family argument: Orin would have been within her rights to demand that Bulik be fined for making unwarranted insinuations.

'If I had said that to *my* wife,' Ayum observed ruefully, 'I would have had to pay twice. First she would have had me fined for making a false accusation, and then she would have had me fined again for adultery, because a remark like that is clear evidence of a guilty conscience.'

All this was little comfort to Bulik who continued to weep long after he had left the longhouse. Our departure should have been made in pouring rain to match the mood, but we left on a pale morning when the transparent mist was powder blue against the sky, and the unseen sun lit the hilltops to golden green. The quiet pool had never looked more inviting nor the longhouse more welcoming. The beach was filled with familiar faces, and as the boat tilted down the rapids my last sight was of dozens of hands waving in farewell.

Down the Bangkit the familiar landmarks repeated their farewells – the green fishing-net caught in the branches, the saffron tree, the longhouse where Danggang told his epic, the clinic, the junction with the Katibas, and at last the wide reaches of the Rejang, with Song perched on the near bank. As we drew in to the jetty, a group of Iban were carrying what at first looked like a rolled-up mat from a boat. On land we discovered that it was the body of a man from the Bangkit who had been crushed to death by a falling log in the timber yard at Bintulu. It was far too serious an omen to be ignored, and Matu and Bulik decided to return to Rumah Langga without delay.

Had we been wise, we should have done the same, but we went instead to the post office where we were expecting a telegram from Tony about our rendezvous for the Batang Ai. The telegram was there, but its message was a bombshell. It said nothing about a rendezvous. With startling inconsistency, Time-Life had decided that the photographs were not satisfactory. They had summoned him back to London immediately for further discussion. I was to follow as soon as possible. There was, according to Tony, no more than 'a fifty-fifty chance' of salvaging the project.

The thunderous ferry to Sibu deadened the shock by making thought impossible, and by the time we reached the Premier Hotel it seemed that something might be rescued. Clearly the T-shirts must have been too intrusive, and Michael thought that at Nanga Bretik it would be easier to get pictures of people in traditional dress. Combined with the traditional exteriors of the Rumah Langga, it would present the image that Lou wanted.

204

Rather to my surprise, Gillian Boucher agreed cautiously to give us a week to see what we could come up with. But the problem ran deeper than T-shirts. The future of the series itself was in question. Orders for Eskimos were disappointing, and for Dinka quite depressing. Perhaps disposable incomes in the valleys of the Ruhr, the Thames and the Po were being hit by recession. Perhaps the market for wildness was saturated. Perhaps – but whatever the reason, management was even now deciding whether to cancel the remainder of the series.

As she spoke I saw spiralling into the distance a succession of people trying to read auguries. I had thought it was simply the three of us in the forest attempting to understand what Lou was telling us in London. But now I saw that Lou had been trying in his turn to read the intentions of the Marketing Department, and they were attempting to appreciate what was on the minds of the middle-class public, who were presumably trying to understand what was happening in the world. At each level, success depended on reading aright the messages from the next level above. The mistake the Iban made was to think that their Singalang Burong was as far as the cosmos went. The truth – at least as it appeared to a divided mind – was that there were Singalang Burongs all the way up.

We had promised to see Ngali again and to visit Ayum's family, and so we decided to take the forlorn hope Gillian had offered and return to the Batang Ai. On the way Ayum lashed out all his wages on a twenty-five horsepower Suzuki outboard. It was at least twice as powerful as he needed for the length of boat and size of river, but he waved these considerations aside. He had been on *bejalai* and he was going to bring back the biggest outboard he could buy. To go with it the salesman gave him a scarlet windcheater and a baseball cap emblazoned with the maker's name, and proudly wearing the colours of his engine he took us up the Batang Ai at top speed.

We passed Ngali tending his fish-traps a few hundred yards from his longhouse. Hero or not a man had to work while he could stand. After we had eaten we went to sit on the gallery,

205

and it was significant that none of those who came to hear what had happened on the Bangkit would trespass on to his mat. It was not Ngali they feared so much as the power of his spirit which could crush theirs if they came too close inadvertently.

In gentle but deadly fashion he and Ayum reminisced about Jingga's *gawai kenyalang*. There had been no discipline, insufficient respect for the effigy, too little glutinous rice for the offerings, the warriors had been improperly dressed, but worst of all was the effigy itself. Proud though Jingga was of his work, he had been unable to produce the sweeping curve of tail and beak which characterises the hornbill. There were hoots of laughter as Ayum sketched out with a gesture the thin straight lines.

'If I had no more than a farmer's saw to work with,' Ngali said contemptuously, 'I could have carved a better one than that.' Then turning to us he said, 'If you want to see what can go wrong with a *gawai kenyalang* go to the Bangkit. But if you want to see it done properly, you must stay on the Batang Ai.'

No doubt the Bangkit Iban would have put it the other way round, but the Batang Ai was where it all began, and in some ways it remained the most traditional in its habits. Yet even as we visited Ngali, a massive hydro-electric dam was being constructed a few miles north of Lubok Antu, which would eventually drown most of the river and twenty-six longhouses including Ngali's.

In the face of such a cataclysm there might seem to be little hope for the Iban of the Batang Ai. The government was planning to resettle them in housing schemes downriver, where the longhouses would be permanent and equipped with electricity and modern comforts all demanding a cash economy.

Permanent longhouses were not uncommon. They had existed for generations on the Saribas river – the first to be settled after the Batang Ai – and ever since the early nineteenth century when they pioneered the trade of piracy, the Iban there had eagerly absorbed the outside world. They were the first to go overseas on *bejalai*, the first to plant rubber and later pepper. It would not be the end of everything if the Batang Ai followed that route. But Limbang pointed to the enduring appeal of the jungle. When we looked in at the Skrang scheme he had already left with Danggang and some others, armed with a chain-saw and enough corrugated iron for a temporary longhouse, which had been bought with Time-Life's wages.

To start a new longhouse was no easy task, but if Limbang needed an example it was to be found at Nanga Bretik. Here the seven families whose longhouse had been burned to the ground were building a new home. Their task was harder than Limbang's for they had lost everything in the fire, jars, gongs, jewellery and blankets. They had, therefore, to remake their past as well. Although the dam would not reach their longhouse they had been offered the chance of moving downriver to the government scheme.

They debated the merits constantly but the attractions of the jungle always won out. That was where the best rice was grown, where pigs and deer could be hunted, and where a longhouse ought to be.

It was difficult to disagree. High up in the hills the air was dry and clear. The stretch of river which the longhouse overlooked was swift and teeming with fish. The fruit trees grew in greater variety and weight than any we had seen, and the rice had a more delicate flavour. The cradle of the Iban migration seemed as good a place as any to begin again.

Ayum was wearing his scarlet Suzuki jacket when we made our departure. The baseball cap was pulled low over his eyes, and he almost stumbled beneath the weight of the enormous engine. Once it was fastened to the transom of the prau, he held out to it a basket of rice and eggs, and muttered a long prayer to its spirit. Then he gently floated the basket away on the current. There was a thunderous roar as we swirled downriver and the offering rocked wildly in our wake. A few hours later we were in Lubok Antu with its fort, its offices and shops. And as we climbed into the bus for Kuching we asked Ayum what sort of reward he wanted for his services.

'A gong,' he said. 'We need a gong to summon the gods.'

Our gods came at the end of a telephone late that night when I called from Kuching. This time their message was unequivocal. Wild People were stopped dead in their tracks. Millions of Time-Life readers would never learn about the Iban, and whether their breasts were bared and their chiefs' nostrils dribbled. Hundreds of thousands of dollars spent on research would have to be written off against tax. And dozens of highly trained employees would have to switch their energies from anthropology to a do-it-yourself car maintenance manual.

A profound and angry misery descended on Michael. He had made many commitments on our behalf and traded heavily on his standing with the Iban to make the book possible. He had been dogged by two people shamelessly drawing on his professional knowledge. The only justification for all this frustration had been the chance of providing the Iban with a platform in the outside world. Now it had all gone for nothing. We had one final explosive row, but his heart was not really in it, and the next day he vanished into the jungle on the Kalimantan side of the border. I don't think I have ever regarded anyone with the same volatile mixture of respect, affection and fury.

With a pang, I felt sure that there was one other victim of the cancellation. For all the effort that he put into the *gawai kenyalang*, it was hard to believe that Jingga's future prosperity was much more securely based than that of the book in which he was to figure. There was, after all, no sound reason for supposing that the auspicious dream which had heralded his festival was any less flawed than Time-Life's market research. Wish-fulfilment was common to both the unitary and divided worlds.

What had brought me to Sarawak was a mistake, but I did not care whether the error was spiritual or statistical. At the crucial moment, a divine or editorial agency had been momentarily blinded, and I slipped through as it blinked the grit from its contact lens. Of course once its sight was restored, the error was bound to be corrected, but for a brief space, the flood of cosmic tears had washed me into paradise.